Healing and Developing our Multiculturalism

Healing and Developing our Multiculturalism

A New Ministry for the Church

WILLIAM J. RADEMACHER

WIPF & STOCK · Eugene, Oregon

HEALING AND DEVELOPING OUR MULTICULTURALISM
A New Ministry for the Church

Copyright © 2009 William J. Rademacher. All rights reserved. Except for brief quotations in critical publications or reviews, no part of this book may be reproduced in any manner without prior written permission from the publisher. Write: Permissions, Wipf and Stock Publishers, 199 W. 8th Ave., Suite 3, Eugene, OR 97401.

Wipf & Stock
A Division of Wipf and Stock Publishers
199 W. 8th Ave., Suite 3
Eugene, OR 97401

www.wipfandstock.com

ISBN 13: 978-1-55635-937-8

Manufactured in the U.S.A.

Unless otherwise noted, Scripture quotations are from the New American Bible. Copyright 1991 by the Confraternity of Christian Doctrine, Washington, DC.

Portions of Appendix II first appeared in María Pilar Aquino, "Theology and Indigenous Cultures of the Americas: Conditions of Dialogue" *CTSA Proceedings* 61 (2006): 19–50; reprinted with the permission of the Catholic Theological Society of America.

To
Bishop Bartolomé De Las Casas
(1484–1566)

Bishop Bartolomé de Las Casas is, without a doubt, the patron saint of multiculturism. In the true prophetic tradition, he defended the dignity and God-given human rights of the poor "Indians" of the Latino peoples. In word and deed he showed respect and reverence for a new culture in spite of, or perhaps because of, its poverty. He spoke truth to power even though that power was wielded by his fellow country-men. He will remain the role model for all Christians who are trying today to build a more human culture in which all cultures are equal before God and country.

May he Rest in Peace.

Contents

Foreword by Bishop Ricardo Ramirez C.S.B. ix
Preface xiii
Introduction xix

1 St. Paul and Multiculturalism 1
2 Meeting the Chinese and the Muslims 10
3 Meeting the Latinos and the Jews 27
4 Diagnosing our Cultures' Wounds 47
5 Anointed to Heal our Cultures' Wounds 83
6 Developing our Cultures 99
7 Our Faith and Inculturation 111
8 An Unsung Prophet 127
9 Conclusions 137

Appendix I: Sacred Memories 141
*Appendix II: Theology and the Indigenous Cultures
                of the Americas 146*
Bibliography 161
Subject/Name Index 165

Foreword

For a modest-sized book, this carries a great wealth of wisdom and draws from a variety of sources: Sacred Scripture, Church tradition, official Church teaching, non-Christian religious faiths, as well as contemporary Latino and Latina theologians and others who write on the relationship between religion and culture.

This is a very timely work, during a period when religion is having such an enormous impact on the contemporary world. The "global village" image is real. Affected by religious forces are not only civil states, but also our immediate communities and our individual lives.

We are rightfully concerned for peace as we see the on-going carnage happening in the Middle East, as well as the threat of terrorism closer to us in the aftermath of 9/11. These are days that try persons' hearts and souls, and we would all do well to examine our consciences, striving to expel everything that is not mercy and love, as well as all racial, ethnic and religious biases. If the world is to survive, it must be filled with people who are passionate about all of us getting along, in spite of our sometimes radical differences.

Dr. Rademacher is correct in pointing out how intertwined culture and religion have always been, and yet how strained the relation between the two can be. It is not only the Roman Catholic Church which, from its beginning, had to confront cultures. As I write this foreword, native Tibetans are in a violent struggle to maintain their religious way of life. Recently, they destroyed a shopping mall filled with Western-made and Western-styled clothing, entertainment and souvenirs, which they saw as affronts to their centuries-old religious and moral values.

Peoples imbued with their cultural traditions can also feel the threat that new religions may bring to their worlds. Dr. Rademacher cites the tensions associated with the evangelization of the Americas in the sixteenth century. Some of these tensions exist even today, especially among ancient indigenous peoples. At times missionaries have tried to impose

Foreword

a new culture because of the belief that the culture they represent goes hand in hand with the religion they are bringing. This is where the challenge of enculturation must be faced.

It is in the theme of enculturation that Dr. Rademacher's work is especially important since the Church of today faces situations that call for a deep understanding and appreciation of cultures if it is to be successful in its missionary efforts. The author's familiarity with the *Decree on the Church's Missionary Activity (Ad Gentes)* contributes generously to this discussion. This section is particularly valuable to the efforts of the Church in the U.S. in meeting the religious and cultural needs of the new immigrants, many of whom are Catholic and most of whom are Latino.

As the Latino communities grow in this country we must find ways of welcoming newcomers. We must allow them to take their rightful place in ministry and to participate in the life of our parishes. We must not tolerate an "*us* and *them*" attitude. We are all "us," because we are all one body with one Lord.

Christianity cannot bless any one culture and claim that it is the only one that can bring its message and be a model for the way of life it upholds. Christianity must bless all cultures and find ways for the Christian message and way of life to be expressed. When cultures are respected and used to convey the Gospel, we all win. The creative genius inherent in Christianity, through the Holy Spirit present within it, will bring forth a refreshing and new way of expressing the message and the living out of the Gospel. An example of this is the way the liturgy of the Eucharist is celebrated throughout the world, even within the norms of the Vatican. In the Far East, where touching others is a sensitive issue, at the sign of peace, people greet each other with a smile and, with hands folded, offer a reverent bow to one other.

But Dr. Rademacher goes beyond the ecclesial or "churchy" issues. He rightly brings into his discourse great issues of our day: peace and war, the ecological question, racism, abortion, and militarism. These issues challenge religion and morality and certainly Christianity. These and other concerns Dr. Rademacher cites in the light of the Second Vatican Council. The author has a keen interest and insight into *The Pastoral Constitution on the Church in the Modern World (Gaudium et Spes)*. His message is a compelling one, especially in his reminder to us that the Church must not be indifferent to the "signs of the times." Rather, it should take these "signs" seriously and respond to them as best it can.

Foreword

    One emphasis in the book which deserves extra attention is the challenge of dialogue. "Dialogue" means not only talking to one another, but also, most importantly, *listening* to one another. Dialogue among different cultural and racial groups is imperative today, as it is among religious communities. Dialogue is also important among other groups: peace activists and militarists, environmentalists and entrepreneurs, advocates for restorative justice and capitalists; consumers and sweat shop workers; health care recipients and HMOs, insurance companies and members of the medical profession.

    This book is as practical as it is insightful. The author has written it so that it will be accessible in both cost and language to the average Catholic. The questions following each chapter will be useful for parish groups, especially for parish pastoral councils. This is a valuable contribution to contemporary discussion on the relationship between religion and culture, and it offers a better understanding of the confusing and bewildering events of our day.

Most Rev. Ricardo Ramírez, C.S.B.
Bishop of Las Cruces

Preface

The Church and Multiculturalism

The sea of Asian faces painted the impression of being in a lively center of Hong Kong. Yet, an unprintable T-shirt in front of us was printed in Spanish. Meanwhile, a person talking loudly on a cell-phone behind us was speaking in heavily accented English. Then two women, dressed head-to-foot in black and covered by abayas, walked by. Though our senses indicated we were touring an exciting, exotic locale, in reality we were waiting at the Los Angeles Airport, where all the world's cultures, it seemed, bustled around us. This experience in the airport is a clear example of the present multicultural context in the United States. In fact, what we witnessed is repeated daily in every airport, shopping mall, and market throughout the country. We have come to a turning point in which the melting point era is giving way to the era of the garden salad bowl. In this new context, immigrant communities maintain continuity with their native cultures, rather than 'melting' into wholly American culture.

Given this new reality, we cannot help but wonder how the Catholic Church should respond. For, at the heart of our faith is the incarnation, in which Jesus Christ, the Lord of all, wholeheartedly embraced the particular Jewish culture of a specific time. He became . . . . This is what we proclaim daily in confessing 'the Word became flesh.' Even more, we believe that the Church, as the body of Christ, is the continuing embodiment of that same Word. The encounter at the Los Angeles airport, which replays itself in a thousand places, poses many serious questions to our Catholic Church. As the "invasion" of immigrants continues, the Church needs to reflect once again on the Word in the scriptures, in its long tradition, and on the Spirit-inspired Word of Vatican II. We need to ask, especially at the parish level, how we should respond to this scene? How can our Church continue to embody Christ with the many surrounding cultures?

Preface

Multiculturalism is only one aspect of our new pluralism. So first, we need to accept today's pluralist reality in our changing world. Pluralism is almost impossible to define, but Roger Haight's is the most helpful. For Haight, pluralism is one aspect of postmodernity:

> ... post-modernity involves a pluralist consciousness. At no other time have people had such a sense of the difference of others, of the pluralism of societies, cultures, and religions, and of the relativity that this entails. One can no longer claim western culture as the center, the higher point of view, or Christianity as the superior religion, or Christ as the absolute center to which all other historical mediations are relative. The world is pluralistic and polycentric in its horizons of interpretation.[1]

In view of all the above, this book is meant to stimulate our Church's reflective process. What in the new cultures are we called to embrace? What, if anything, are we called to exorcize? Do we actively shape and develop the new cultures? Or, do we passively accept and bless whatever the new cultures bring with them? How do we initiate a process of prayerful discernment with our new people? How do we learn the art of listening non-judgmentally to their new story? Do we cooperate uncritically with our governments, whether local or federal? Or, do we go our own way? What do we mean when, on the feast of the Epiphany, we sing: "Lord every nation on earth will adore you?" Implicit in all of these questions is the more challenging question: how do our Church and our parishes relate to the changing world around it?

The fact of enculturation is not new to our Church; but the forms and methods of enculturation have to be new because the cultures are new. History is not cyclic, as has often been assumed: it does not always repeat itself in the same way. After the invention of the automobile, the atomic bomb, the computer, and the cell phone, history and its cultures will never be the same. Rather, History is dialectic in that it is always in a process of action and reaction. Besides, after Vatican II, the Church, as a living body, will never be the same. So, the relationships and the interactions of Church and culture will be in a constant state of adjustment to new conditions. The two bodies will be in a constant state of true dialogue that leads to the discovery of that which is radically new.

---

1. Haight, *Jesus, Symbol of God*, 333.

Preface

We may catch a glimpse of the intersection of cultures in the earliest stages of the life of the Church. In the Jerusalem Church, the Greek-speaking widows were being neglected in the daily distribution (Acts 6). Of course, in the patriarchal Jewish culture widows, having lost their husbands, were at the very bottom rung of the social ladder. But was that kind of inequality and discrimination going to continue in the new Christian Church? No way, said the Greek-speaking widows. They raised their voices in protest. They "murmured" loud enough to draw the attention of the apostles. It was a very Jewish Church in Jerusalem at that time, yet there was a language division between the Aramaic-speaking Christian Jews and the diaspora Christian Jews who had returned to Jerusalem, probably from Alexandria where they spoke Greek.

So how did the Church respond? It created a new ministry, choosing seven indigenous leaders to minister in the daily distribution to the poor Greek-speaking widows. But they were not restricted to waiting on tables. A little later, in Acts 6, we see Stephen, one of the seven, doing "great wonders and signs among the people;" and, Philip "went down to a city in Samaria and proclaimed to them the Christ." Like the apostles, "the seven" new ministers went out "preaching the word." It was plain that the Greek language was not going to be an obstacle in the Jewish Church. The new Christian Church, although born in a thoroughly Jewish culture, was not going to be bound to any one culture: it was going to be multicultural. And so it must always be if it is going to be an effective sign of the Kingdom of God.

A BRIEF WORD TO OUR IMMIGRANTS

Welcome! Legal or illegal: welcome! My wife, who is from Guatemala, and I embrace you with the kiss of peace. We hope and pray you will receive the Christian hospitality you rightly deserve. We hope you will find at least part of the "Promised Land" you are seeking. We are both sorry you will have to climb that mountain of bureaucracy to obtain citizenship. At the same time, we hope and pray you will not get discouraged.

Even more, we hope you will help us heal the wounds in our multiculturalism. We also hope you will assimilate into our culture with critical and prayerful discernment, sifting the wheat from the chaff. The pathologies of our culture will test your compassion for human frailty. We trust you will also rejoice at our virtues. But your painful journey so far has

Preface

prepared you to make your own unique contributions to our cultures. We are richer for your presence. We hope you find the jobs you need to feed your families so that you may enjoy freedom from hunger. We hope you participate in our democracy, such as it is: no doubt it will become better through your active participation. You are now singing as "a free people walking through the waters of life, a free people with great faith and religion." (*Pueblo libre caminando por las aguas . . . con gran fe y religion*). We hope you can soon join us in singing: "Oh God let all the nations praise your name."

A Word of Thanks

As this book goes to press I want to thank Dr. David McNamara and Mr. Richard Petrillo of the Las Cruces Diocesan Pastoral Center for their careful, critical reading of the text. Their comments and suggestions were extremely helpful in clarifying both style and content. And I want to thank John Andrews, the former director of Inter-library Loan at our Branigan Library, Las Cruces, NM. If the book I needed was in print, he would move heaven and earth to find it. Many thanks to Angelica Webster for teaching me the mysteries of Microsoft Word. I am deeply grateful to Carrie Wolcott, my editor at Wipf and Stock, for her patience with my many delays in getting the final manuscript to her desk. I'm sure all my readers join me in expressing deep gratitude to Michael Wicks, my copy editor. He improved the text immeasurably for easier and, indeed, more enjoyable reading.

I owe a large debt of gratitude to Bishop Ricardo Ramirez, Bishop of the Diocese of Las Cruces, for taking time out from his busy schedule to write the Foreword. But I am especially grateful that the Bishop read the whole manuscript so carefully he even found a mistake in the footnotes. I would not sleep at night if that mistake had gone off to the publisher.

Finally, I want to thank my wife for her patience while I was "married" to my books and to my computer. Without the gracious cooperation of many friends, this book would remain nothing more than a dream in my head.

In the autumn years of my life I am also grateful to God that I had the opportunity to travel to experience many other cultures in my younger years. From the wonderful people of China, Korea, Europe, Mexico and Guatemala I learned more about different cultures than I could ever learn from books. There were many passing encounters with real, live, gracious, native peoples. These encounters were the doors and windows through which, for one precious, fleeting moment, I could see and experience their history and culture.

I remember the Japanese lady, who, with a smile and profound bow, welcomed me as I stepped into the elevator at a Tokyo hotel. I recall the smiling old man who got on his hands and knees to help me look for a piece of my watch which I lost on a cracked sidewalk in Guatemala City. I can still hear the sad voice of the lady in charge of a small family store near my bus stop in Mazatlan, Mexico, when she said *lo siento, no tengo*: "I'm sorry I have no donuts left this morning." And I will never forget the elderly man in the park in Munich, Germany, who, when I asked him for directions in my "fluent" German, he answered with a broad smile in perfect English. In New Delhi, India, our bus driver stopped and waited with patience, almost reverence, as a sacred cow, slowly, ever so slowly, walked across our highway. He turned to smile at us Americans who didn't know why he was stopping for a cow. In Seoul, South Korea, all the caddies at the golf course were young ladies. I was embarrassed that a lady would have to carry my clubs. "That's part of their culture," commented my Maryknoll companion. It was also a brief glimpse into the misogyny running through the Korean culture. But in my many travels I learned that the unspoken language of smiles and tears crosses all cultures instantly.

Introduction

THE SECOND VATICAN COUNCIL was a wonderful turning point in the history of our Church, especially for us oldsters, who were accustomed to the pre-conciliar top-down ecclesiology. This event was much more than Pope John XXIII's "open window:" it was, indeed, the "wonders of a New Pentecost," which the Pope had prayed for. When we first read the *Dogmatic Constitution on the Church* and then *The Pastoral Constitution of the Church in the Modern World,* we could not help but sing a triple 'alleluia.' How refreshing it was to see that the Council put the People of God **first** in the *Dogmatic Constitution on the Church*. But it was even more exciting that the Council turned its attention *ad extra* to the Church in the modern World.

The purpose of this book is to invite the reader to reflect, and, indeed, pray over the pastoral implications of that wonderful document: *The Pastoral Constitution on the Church in the Modern World*. This is our Church *ad extra*. And, for most of us, this is an orientation of our Church that is totally new.

We start this book with some reflections on the Word of God as it comes to us through St. Paul's letters. How would St. Paul respond, in word and deed, to the multicultural condition of our modern day setting? How would he react to today's many indigenous peoples? How would he plant the seeds of the Gospel in the contemporary proliferation of new cultures?

Following reflection on the letters of St. Paul, we will examine some historical examples of encounters between the Church and other cultures (e.g., Chinese and Muslim). From here, we will turn to the relationship of the Church with Jewish and Latino cultures. These points will lead us to the question of our responsibility to these different cultures in the light of the Gospel and *The Pastoral Constitution on the Church in the Modern World*. And, likewise, the corresponding question is raised: what do these cultures do to us? Can we, the Church, accept these cultures as the Church once accepted the culture of the Roman Empire, including its legal sys-

Introduction

tem? How do we, the people of God, sift the wheat from the chaff as we encounter these new cultures?

It is always an exciting experience to look at the inner workings of the Church, though it continues to be a mystery in both its structures and its mission. Examining the interior of the Church is somewhat like looking at the insides of a combine or threshing machine: we are amazed at all the complicated machinery. But, immediately, we ask what all this machinery is for? We get our answer when we see the machine in action. Similarly, we get our answer regarding the Church when we see the Church in action relating to the outside world, feeding the hungry, clothing the naked and welcoming the immigrants etc. Now it is even more exiting, since Vatican II, to see the Church relating in a more positive way to God's created, but wounded world. God is present in a variety of ways in the world He created, but it is up to us, under the guidance of the Holy Spirit, to discern that presence in our own time, and "read the signs of the times." God, our Creator, will be present in His creation in more ways than we assume.

Nevertheless, a close look at our world and its cultures will also discover some wounds that need healing. And, since the *Pastoral Constitution*, we know that all of us have a unique vocation to develop the world God is co-creating with us. We all respond to the baptismal call: "Here I am Lord, send me." (Is 6:8). But, our response demands that we be equipped for the task; that is, that we know how to apply the Word we hear on Sunday to the real conditions in this world. This book is meant to be part of our equipment in ministering to a broken world. As we go into the Lord's vineyard, we lean more on God's grace than on our human talents. But God can, and does, accomplish wonders through clay instruments like ourselves. Our world may not know it, but our world is waiting. The gracious hospitality of the Maryknollers during my journeys through the East will be embedded in my aging memory until my pall-bearers come. Without their guidance, I would have been nothing more than a passing tourist. Thanks be to God, they enriched my journey immeasurably. This book is, at least partly, the fruit of that experience. I hope and pray it will move many readers toward a deeper respect, indeed reverence, for the many new cultures coming here now from far off lands to be our dear neighbors.

1

St. Paul and Multiculturalism

Multiculturalism, as noted in the Introduction, is not a new challenge for the Catholic Church. The New Testament, especially St. Paul's letters and Luke-Acts, reveals numerous encounters with a variety of cultures. These scriptures will be our first guide in dealing with the contemporary intersection of cultures. We look to the scriptures, however, not as laws, but for inspiration, as a source of insights, to shed the light of God's Word on some of today's pastoral problems and garner a possible response. For the sake of brevity, we will concentrate primarily on Paul's seven authentic letters.

The Apostle Paul was born as Saul around the year 1 B.C.E. in Tarsus, Cilicia, Asia Minor. He was born and raised as a strict practitioner of the Jewish faith. Being a diaspora Jew from Tarsus did not dilute his Jewishness or his zeal for the teachings of the Torah. At that time it was customary to combine the study of the Torah with some kind of trade: Saul became a tent-maker. Through his occupation as a tent-maker, Saul was exposed to a variety of cultures. Tarsus was a large, prosperous and cosmopolitan city, and some of Saul's customers may well have been members of the Roman military, as well as travelers from various foreign countries. His interactions with those for whom he toiled likely broadened his understanding and appreciation of the vast network of cultures running throughout the ancient near eastern world.

Not much is known about Saul's domestic life except his occupation. Saul probably began his trade as an apprentice in his father's workshop at age thirteen. Describing the likely conditions of his daily life, Pauline scholar Ronald Hock comments that "making tents meant rising before dawn, toiling until sunset with leather, knives, and awls, and accepting the various social stigmas and humiliations that were part of the artisans lot, not to mention the poverty—being cold, hungry, and poorly clothed."[1] In his father's shop Saul worked elbow to elbow with the slaves. Yet, his hard work in the sweaty world of the tentmaker posed no conflict with his deep spirituality and his strict practice of the Jewish religion.

A passionate man to the core, Saul was never half-hearted about anything. In 32 C.E. he began to persecute the Christians with great zeal. He watched the stoning of St. Stephen, the Christian Church's first martyr, with approval: "And Saul was consenting to his death" (Acts 8:1). Understandably, following Stephen's stoning, many Christians fled the Jerusalem area, some escaping to Damascus. But Saul, with violent intentions, chased after the fleeing Christians in the hope of capturing them and taking them back to Jerusalem.

He was on his way to Damascus when "a light from heaven flashed about him," and "His eyes were opened" (Acts 9:8). Whatever the historicity of the details in Acts, Saul experienced a profound, perhaps gradual, religious conversion. From being a zealous persecutor of Christians, Saul became a zealous preacher of the Christian message of the Word of God. In fact, he became an important pillar in the new Christian Church, proclaiming the Gospel to Jews and Gentiles alike, undertaking a set of vast missionary enterprises.

In these events, we are confronted with the question of how Saul, who took the name Paul following his conversion, dealt with the wide variety of cultures he encountered on his missionary journeys. The scandalous morals of Greek Corinth were far removed from the strict Judaism of Saul, the Pharisee. And how did the new Paul deal with the cultural gulf between Antioch and Galilee? "Antioch," writes Edward Stourton "was a mix of self-conscious chic and unabashed pagan polytheism, culturally, if not geographically, a world away from the hills of Galilee."[2] Rome too was a capital of polytheism with as many pagan temples as New York has McDonald's golden arches.

CULTURE DEFINED

But before we try to answer the above questions we need to have a working definition of "culture." It can be a slippery word. First of all, culture is not the same as race. We are born into a specific race without choice or

---

1. Ronald F. Hock, *The Social Context of Paul's Ministry*, 37.
2. Stourton, *Paul of Tarsus*, 64.

ability to alter it as a fact. Secondly, culture is not the same as ethnicity, which usually refers to a nationality or minority group. Yet, race, ethnicity and culture are very much intertwined. We will begin with the definition of culture given by Vatican II's *Pastoral Constitution on the Church in the Modern World*: "The word 'culture' in its general sense indicates all those factors by which man refines and unfolds his manifold spiritual and bodily qualities."[3] "Culture" used in this sense is fairly new in church documents, in that it is a departure from older documents that defined culture from a specifically Catholic or Christian standpoint. The Council here accepts a positive understanding of secular culture more in tune with the social sciences of the time, which perceive that culture is very much the product of human labor and ingenuity. Culture, so understood, can be seen to consist of an "historical and social" aspect, as the *Pastoral Constitution* reminds us.

Still by way of definition, it may be helpful, with John Kavanaugh, to look at culture, from a threefold perspective:

> *A culture is a cult.* It is a revelation system. It is the entire range of corporate ritual, of symbolic forms, human expressions, and productive systems. It quietly converts, elicits commitments, transforms, provides heroics, and suggests human fulfillments. The culture, then, is a gospel—a book of revelation—mediating beliefs, revealing us to ourselves. *A culture is cultivation.* Humans tend and till themselves through nature into culture ... although culture is made by humans, in a special manner it makes us–to some extent in its own image. *A culture is a corporate symbolic dwelling place*...the culture is a human tabernacle, the incarnation of corporate spirit ... culture is *of* psyche and psyche is formed *by* culture ... Culture is the product of men and women.[4]

A choice is given to us regarding our relationship to culture. We can be passive, as mere bystanders and sometimes even as victims, or we can be active as participants and builders. We can make our customs, institutions and social life more human both within the family and in the civic community. "The role of Catholics is to participate in and to act as a leaven

---

3. Walter M. Abbot, S.J., ed. *The Documents of Vatican II*, [DVII] (New York: America Press, 1966), no. 59. [All references to Vatican II documents will be to the numbers in the text correspondent with the Flannery edition.

4. Kavanaugh, *Following Christ in a Consumer Society*, 80. [Italics mine].

Healing and Developing our Multiculturalism

within the many cultures of the modern world."[5] If we don't develop our culture, our culture will develop us. If we are passive before our culture, we will become clay in the hands of the potter. By osmosis or by its daily media onslaught, culture will mold and shape us in it own image, with its own values, with its own clay heroes as models. If we don't actively take a counter-cultural stand, if we don't become the salt and the yeast in our culture, we will become dust blowing in the wind. So we need to cling tenaciously to the risen Christ in order to hang on to our very Christian identity. And, as we will see with St. Paul, it can be done.

Our own U.S. culture is presently so fluid and evolving so rapidly into multiculturalism it tends to resist a precise definition. Dr. Victor Davis Hanson, of California State University, gives us a passing glimpse of this phenomenon: "The only requisites for success in this glitzy culture are charm, athleticism, looks and pizzazz—none of it the property of any one ethnicity. If a Latina is curvy, she not only captures more attention than a rail-thin white woman ... but wins commensurate money, status and celebrity ..."[6] In light of this, we must take caution, while reviewing Paul's encounters with the cultures of his day, not to retroject our present "glitzy" and evolving U.S. culture unto Paul's time. On the other hand, we may discern some helpful general principles in Paul's pastoral style that give us some hints on how to respond to, and perhaps change, our multicultural society. We will list some of today's pastoral problems and then see how Paul's seven authentic letters shed some light on a possible pastoral response.

PAUL AND OUR IMMIGRANTS, LEGAL OR ILLEGAL

Paul's seven letters can indeed be a helpful guide in dealing with our millions of immigrants. But first we may need to take a prophetic stand with respect to some of the blind prejudices that are deeply rooted in our own culture. We won't see clearly if the beams within our own culture obstruct our sight. For instance, we are not a better culture because we have running water and others do not; or, because we have the latest TV or iPods and others do not.

At the beginning of his letter, Paul states his position regarding other cultures quite clearly in Rom 1:14–16: "I am under obligation both to Greeks and to barbarians, both to the wise and to the foolish: so I am

---

5. Tanner, *The Church and the World*, 75.
6. Hanson, *Mexifornia*, 137.

eager to preach the Gospel also to you who are in Rome." Making his case more emphatically, Paul asks: "Is God the God of Jews only? Is He not the God of Gentiles also? Yes, of Gentiles also, since God is one" (Rom 3:29–30). Given the context in the Roman church, where Christian Jews and Gentiles lived together, Paul highlights "Abraham who is the father of us all, the father of many nations" (Rom 4:16–17). The law was for the Jews; but faith goes beyond the law and includes all nations, and all cultures. In view of the Gospel and Jesus' death for all humans, we are under obligation without exception to proclaim the Gospel to all, even to the "foolish and to the barbarians."

Further, Paul tells us "God shows no partiality"; there will be "glory and honor and peace for everyone who does well, the Jew first and also the Greek" (Rom 2:10–11). These passages demonstrate quite clearly that one culture is not preferred to another before God, nor is one more worthy or meritorious. We may deduce from this that we are to think well of every new culture that comes across our borders. Paul goes further than this, even, and gives an injunction to the Romans that they are "to practice hospitality" (Rom 12:13). What Paul has in mind here is likely the command given to the Israelites in the Pentateuch: "When an alien settles with you in your land, you shall not oppress him. He shall be treated as a native born among you, and you shall love him as a man like yourself, because you were aliens in Egypt. I am the Lord your God" (Lev 19: 33–34). In the present, parish communities who publicly proclaim this Word of God in their churches need to welcome all new cultures, however strange their customs may seem to their hosts. Given his directives to the Romans, we can conclude with some certainty that Paul would not support building a seven hundred mile fence along the U. S. / Mexico border. More likely he would offer the "ministry of reconciliation" to our southern neighbors crossing the border (2 Cor 5:18–19).

In the letter to the Galatians, Paul recounts his disagreement with Peter (2:11). At its deepest level this fight was really about the proper attitude of the early Church toward the Jews and the Gentiles, which were two very different cultures. Should the Jewish law and circumcision be required of the new Gentile converts or not? Peter appeared to straddle the fence on this issue: when those of the party who held strictly to these rules were not around, he ate with the Gentiles, presumably breaking the Jewish dietary laws; but, when the Jews came from James, the pillar in Jerusalem, Peter separated himself and refused to eat with the Gentiles. On account of this behavior, Paul scolded Peter for his insincerity, saying directly to Peter's face: "If you, though a Jew, live like a Gentile and not like a Jew, how can you compel the Gentiles to live like Jews?" (Gal 2:14). Unlike the wavering and inconsistency of Peter, Paul argues straightforwardly: "For as many of you as were baptized into Christ have put on Christ. *There is neither Jew nor Greek, there is neither slave nor free, there is neither male nor female; for you are all one in Christ Jesus*" (Gal 3:27–28).

Appropriately, these powerful words have been quoted often throughout the centuries. But most importantly, they helped form the foundation of the early Church: Jews and Gentiles are now welcome to share the cup and break bread at the same table. With this kind of foundation the early church would explode into the Gentile world. From now on all cultures are "one in Christ Jesus." The reference to baptism clinches Paul's argument; for, baptism applies the grace of the redeeming blood of Christ to all cultures. So now through baptism into Christ distinctions like race, ethnicity and culture simply disappear. After the Resurrection, no nation or earthly institution can put boundaries on the risen Christ's saving grace.

PAUL'S INDIGENOUS LEADERS

In January 2006 Bolivia elected its first indigenous president in history. President Evo Morales, as a native Indian, represents the 60% of Bolivia's Indian population whose culture goes back to 500 B.C. E. Thousands of indigenous people celebrated the beginning of a new era in Bolivia. Morales's election marked the beginning of the end of the exploitation of Bolivia's natural resources, first by Spain and then by other Western countries. Tens of thousands of Indians rejoiced because President Morales was "one of their own." They felt in the depth of their hearts that their unique culture deserved its very own indigenous leadership.

Paul, in spite of his strict Jewish upbringing, applied the same principle of indigenous leadership in his missionary journeys into the Gentile world. A new Christian culture, he felt, deserved a leadership it could call its very own. The endings of Paul's letters reveal that he selected quite a few leaders, couriers and companions—both men and women—to help him in his pastoral work (there are twenty-six such persons mentioned in Romans alone.) Timothy, a frequent companion of Paul, was a Gentile, a native of Lystra in Lycaonia. He was born of a Gentile father and Jewish mother. Paul selected him to be the leader of a very troubled Church in

Ephesus. Titus was a Gentile convert who was charged with establishing the Church in Crete, a large Mediterranean island Paul had never visited.

We cannot omit Phoebe, the deaconess, who had a pastoral leadership role in the Church of Cenchreae, a port city about seven miles from Corinth (Rom 16:1). Besides her duties as a deaconess, she evidently served as a courier, probably carrying Paul's letter to Rome. While it is true that Paul uses the Greek, *diakonos*, which is masculine, the masculine form at that time was often used in a generic sense for all kinds of service. The feminine Greek form did not come into use until later in the Patristic period. What is important in this is that Paul gives women an important leadership role in the early Church. This is a little surprising since both the Greek and the Roman cultures were unabashedly patriarchal in their governments and social organization. Yet, it is clear that Paul believes strongly in indigenous and inclusive leadership. This is certainly based upon the same principle that guided his thought in regard to the questions of ethnicity and culture, namely that all categories which previously divided people from each other are erased in Christ through our baptism. We may conclude from this, with Paul, that after the Resurrection *gender can no longer be an issue in selecting leaders,* even in patriarchal cultures. The risen Christ, now transformed, transcends earthly genders.

THE COLLECTION FOR THE SAINTS IN JERUSALEM

We simply cannot overlook the theological significance of Paul's collection for "the saints in Jerusalem" (1 Cor 16:1-4). In 44-48 C.E., under Tiberius Alexander, there was a severe famine in Jerusalem. Word came to the Gentile Christians in Antioch that the Jewish Christians in Jerusalem were suffering from hunger. For Paul, unity within the community of all the baptized was a fundamental principle of the new Christian religion. His frequent use of the image of the Body of Christ is especially pertinent here: if one part of the body suffers hunger, then so do the other parts. Therefore, Paul took up a collection among the Gentile Christians for the starving Jewish Christians in Jerusalem. The collection was a powerful symbol of the unity that ought to exist between the diverse Jewish and Gentile cultures. As well, this collection was consistent with Paul's conception of one true community of all the baptized whatever their culture; and, on this basis, Paul did not hesitate to call the new Christian community the true Israel. "In using this expression," writes Keith Nickle,

"[Paul] was intentionally cutting across all the ethnic, social, and cultic distinctions which were of such determinative importance for 'Israel after the flesh.'"[7] When the Jewish Christians accepted the collection from the Gentile Christians they were agreeing that the baptized Gentiles now were equal members with them in the new Christian community: in the risen Christ two very distinct cultures became one.

DIVISIONS IN THE CHURCH AT CORINTH

There is an instructive warning in 1 Cor 3: 5–11 for those who cling to their native cultures so tenaciously so as to cause divisions within the Christian community. Paul is, in fact, quite disturbed by divisions in the Church of Corinth, and scolds the Corinthians for their "jealousy and strife." Apparently, the Corinthian community was divided internally among factions fiercely loyal to a particular figure: on one side were those identified with Paul and on the other with Apollos. Raising a series of questions, Paul teaches an important lesson: "Who then is Apollos? Who is Paul? Servants, through whom you believed, as the Lord assigned to each. I planted, Apollos watered, but God gave the growth . . . he who plants and he who waters are equal . . . For we are all God's fellow workers: you are God's field, God's building . . . For no other foundation can anyone lay than that which is laid, which is Jesus Christ" (1 Cor 3:5–9).

Just as there are no borders in Christ's Body so there are no borders in "God's building." No building can stand when one part is disjointed from the other. More importantly, we cannot cling to God's human servants, however charming, charismatic or indigenous, to the detriment of the foundation of unity which will always be Jesus Christ, though the very human temptation to cling to an indigenous messenger rather than to the message which is Jesus Christ will always be with us.

It is quite significant that Paul, after listing the variety of gifts given by the Spirit (1 Cor 12:12), returns to his favorite image of the Body of Christ: "For just as the body is one and has many members, and all the members of the body, though many, are one body, so it is with Christ. For by one Spirit we were all baptized into one body—Jews or Greeks, slaves or free—and all were made to drink of one Spirit." In keeping with the Body image, Paul does not condition or limit the distribution of gifts by gender or culture; for, the Spirit's gifts transcend gender and cultures.

---

7. Nickle, *The Collection*, 116.

St. Paul and Multiculturalism

We can conclude from this brief and highly selective review of Paul's authentic letters that in the Body of Christ there are no borders. Once baptized, both sides of the border have their place at the Lord's Table of fellowship, and the Christians on either side of whatever border call those on the other side their sisters and brothers. They pray and sing with one voice to praise the one God before whom no race, color, or culture is outside of His love. But we still need to review how the Church has applied Paul's teaching through its long, and indeed, checkered history. Both interculturation and enculturation will be an ongoing process in every Christian community.

There remain many other serious modern questions regarding multiculturalism which Paul does not answer. How does a Christian bread-breaking community relate to the so-called secular culture around it? Is it called to build a totally new culture? Or, does it form a separate, ghetto culture? Does it assimilate into the existing secular culture? Will there be many distinct cultures, each clinging to Christ in its own traditional culture? Or, will there be a new melting pot in which Christians will be the salt and the yeast for a single but totally new culture? How does the Christian community maintain its unity and, at the same time, deal with the language barrier? What, finally, can we learn from the Church's long history in dealing with a great variety of cultures? The following chapters will try to deal briefly with some of these complicated issues.

QUESTIONS FOR DISCUSSION

1. To what extent does our culture "make us into its own image?"
2. How would St. Paul respond to the undocumented immigrants coming into our country?
3. How do you react to Kavanaugh's saying "Culture is the product of men and women?"
4. Does the lay leadership in your parish, including your parish council, reflect your multiculturalism?
5. In what ways do you take a prophetic, counter-cultural stand? In your community? Your state?
6. How would St. Paul deal with the multiculturalism in your parish? Your community?
7. How do you apply St. Paul's principle of indigenous leadership in your own parish? Recall Phoebe in the Church of Cenchreae.

2

Meeting the Chinese and the Muslims

Thomas Edison had many failures before he discovered the right filament for his electric light bulb. However, each failure was a learning opportunity. Champion athletes also fail many times before they bring home an Olympic gold medal. For them every failure, as for Edison, contains within itself an occasion for improvement, ultimately leading toward success.

Our Church, throughout its long history, has had many failures in dealing with other cultures. In hindsight, and, with the benefit of history, we become more aware of these failures. Simultaneously, we also recognize, and indeed, celebrate the many successes of the Church. As a living body, the Church learns and grows through both successes and failures. These experiences can be signs of the Holy Spirit's presence in the Church, mysteriously leading it through this earthly pilgrimage.

In order to understand the tasks facing the Church in the present time, it is necessary to gain an appreciation of the current context of the Church in the United States—a situation that is not aptly reflected even in the revised *Catechism of the Catholic Church*. By perceiving the extent of the cultural diversity in our time, we may then begin to see the connections with and the lessons to be learned from the past through which we might discover new ways of interacting with the various cultures of our present context. Of fundamental importance in the present situation is the need for an awareness of *all* the cultural inhabitants of our space; for, while we are increasingly aware of the growing Latino/a culture in the U.S., we must not neglect "the 2.5 million Asian and Pacific Islander Catholics now living in the U.S." Besides these Catholics, the 2000 U.S. census reports that there are approximately "1.5 million Filipinos, 325,000 Vietnamese, 300 Chinese, 285,000 Indians, 74,000 Koreans, 48,000 Guamanians, 31,000

Meeting the Chinese and the Muslims

Japanese, 20,000 Samoans, and 4000 Tongans"[1] living in the U.S. In other words, our garden salad of "new" cultures has a much greater variety than most of us assume. Therefore, the process of enculturation will have a broad application: it cannot be limited to a specific culture or religion. Different cultures are often the bearers of different religions, and each religion may be one window into its particular culture. Each religion, additionally, has to be an active partner in the process of enculturation. Anything less than this would be a denial of the teaching in Vatican II's Declaration, *Nostra Aetate*. In this historic document "the Church affirms that all peoples on the earth with their various religions form one community; the Church respects the spiritual, moral, and cultural values of Hinduism, Buddhism, and Islam."[2] Yet we should not assume from this that all religions should be melted into one, for infinite mystery will always be revealed in a variety of finite earthly forms.

OUR CHURCH IN CHINA (1582–1742)

Aspects of the Chinese culture are increasingly visible in the milieu of today's multicultural society. For instance, it is commonplace to hear the Chinese language spoken in the marketplace, the everyday commodities in our shopping carts often bear the label 'manufactured in China,' and the signage in our public spaces are inscribed with Chinese characters. Within the context of such visible cultural growth, Americans increasingly are seeking to educate themselves about Chinese culture, as we see, for example, courses in the Chinese language being offered in our educational institutions. At the same time, many in our society are more comfortable embracing the abstract reality of China as a nation assuming a significant role on the world stage than accepting the presence of the Chinese as neighbor.

While the present day sees a visibly strong, engaged China on the global stage, this was not always the case. In 1583, a Jesuit priest named Matteo Ricci launched the second Catholic missionary expedition into mainland China. What he saw was an ancient, yet restricted and closed civilization. A Spanish missionary who had tried to visit China com-

---

1. Fox, "U.S. Asian Catholics Gather in D.C.," *The National Catholic Reporter*, (14 July 2006) 9.

2. Robert A. Graham, Introduction to *Nostra Aetate*, in DVII, 658.

plained: "with or without soldiers, to try to enter China is like trying to reach the moon."[3]

But before we make any assessments of the success or failure of this Jesuit mission into the Chinese culture, we need to determine what kind of Catholic missionary principles were put into effect at that time. How do we measure success or failure? What criteria do we apply to the missionary activities of the Church in the Chinese culture? Correspondingly, how do we reach any conclusions that may apply to the Church's response to multiculturalism today? What failed in 1583 may succeed today and vice versa. Nevertheless, we need to find out what theological principles, implicit or explicit, were in effect when our Western Church encountered this totally "new" culture in the Far East.

Within their missionary efforts, the ancient principle of "missionary accommodation" was well known and practiced by the Jesuit missionaries at that time. Even though the degree of accommodation was a matter of controversy among religious orders, the principle itself was not. That principle was clearly contained in the instructions issued by the Vatican in 1659. Even though these specific instructions were issued 75 years after the Jesuits arrived in China, there is considerable evidence that the Jesuits, like St. Paul before them, practiced the same missionary accommodation much earlier.

The pertinent Vatican instruction is here quoted at some length because of its quasi- permanent validity:

> Do not regard it as your task, and do not bring any pressure to bear on the peoples, to change their manners, customs and uses, unless they are evidently contrary to religion and sound morals. What could be more absurd than to transplant France, Spain, Italy or some other European country to China? Do not introduce all that to them but only the faith, which does not despise or destroy the manners and customs of any people, always supposing that they are not evil, but rather wishes to see them unharmed ... It is the nature of men to love and treasure above everything else their own country and that which belongs to it ... Do not draw invidious contrasts between the customs of the peoples and those of Europe; do your utmost to adapt yourselves to them.[4]

---

3. Gonzalez, *Story of Christianity*, 407.
4. Quoted in Paul Johnson, *A History of Christianity*, 414.

Meeting the Chinese and the Muslims

This Vatican instruction, of course, is primarily concerned about what not to do. It could hardly include what specific customs in the new culture should be blessed and accepted by our Church. It would be up to the missionaries themselves to decide. Making such a determination, the missionaries were expected to cling fast to their own identity and the identity of the Catholic Church they represent. For, they bring with them the Good News of the Gospel, the Nicene Creed, the seven sacraments and life everlasting in the risen Christ. Given this constant, the missionaries were faced with the question of what in the new culture was compatible with the saving truths the Lord entrusted to those who proclaim the Gospel? We know already that our timeless and unbounded God is certainly present in every new culture long before any missionaries arrive. The question arises, how and in what forms, is He present? No doubt evil, in its various and mysterious forms, is also present. Sometimes it is present in the many forms of superstition and idolatry.

We need to note, before we proceed further, that in our Church there is a tremendous difference between dogma and discipline. For instance, the law of celibacy is a discipline in the Latin rite only since The Second Lateran Council (1139). In contrast, the Incarnation of Jesus Christ, from the beginning of Christianity, is an unchangeable dogma to be believed by all cultures and countries. It is one of many of our saving truths. This dogma is a constitutive part of the Good News. The specific language of the Eucharist is a discipline. Eucharistic and liturgical language can be varied and even changed within different cultural settings. Thus, in 1615, Pope Paul V authorized a Chinese Liturgy, centuries before the liturgical changes approved at the Second Vatican Council (1962–65). But even the truths of unchangeable dogma can be expressed in new language and symbols so long as the original meaning is retained. So, the theological principle of accommodation can have wide application both in disciplinary and in dogmatic teaching. The unity of the Church can be preserved through universal dogma, the Creeds, rituals and the Liturgy. The *heart of the Eucharist*, the breaking of the Bread of the Lord, is a real symbol with a unifying dynamic that *transcends all cultures*.

THE JESUITS IN CHINA

We have numerous examples of the Jesuits practicing accommodation in China in accordance with the boundaries noted above. The brilliant

Mateo Ricci was the recognized leader of the Jesuit mission to China. Well-versed in the Confucian classics, he gained considerable respect from his dialogues with Confucian scholars. He studied the Confucian teachings and translated them into Latin. He made a chiming clock and a harpsichord and presented them as gifts to the emperor. Once he discovered how important friendship was to the Chinese, he wrote a treatise on friendship, thereby gaining great esteem among the upper classes. In addition to these achievements, he was a geographer, astronomer, mathematician and clockmaker. Ricci used these talents in his interactions with Chinese culture with a sense of openness; for instance, even though Catholic Europe thought the world was only 5000 years old, Ricci learned from Chinese chronology that the world was much older than that.

Once he understood Confucian philosophy, Ricci explored the areas of agreement with Christian teaching: "the existence of a personal God, immortality of the soul and eternal reward or punishment."[5] Ricci made a clear distinction between Confucianism and Buddhism. The latter, he decided, was filled with idolatry and superstition. But Ricci was sure one did not have to give up Confucianism or reject the Chinese culture in order to be a good Christian. Regarding Chinese ancestor worship, Ricci "claimed that this was not true worship, but rather, a social custom whereby one showed respect for one's ancestors."[6] Ricci, in fact, used the same word for the Mass as the Chinese used for ancestor "worship." But these and other controversial adaptations would eventually cause trouble for Ricci and his Jesuit companions with Rome.

By 1664, there were many indications that the Jesuit mission into the Chinese culture was fruitful both for the Church and for China: it is reported that there were 254,980 converts. Through this, it began to appear that the Catholic Church was finally on its way to becoming a 'world religion.' The Jesuits, through dialogue and humanist interaction, built many positive relationships with the Chinese and their culture. In 1601, for instance, Matteo Ricci received the rare honor of being invited to the imperial court, where he received the funds to build an observatory in Beijing. With few exceptions the principle of adaptation and accommodation seemed to be working rather well. It was a bridge that provided mutual enrichment for both the Catholic Church and the Chinese culture.

5. Ronald Modras, *Ignatian Humanism*, 113. I owe a great debt of gratitude to Dr. Modras for his extensive, in-depth research on Matteo Ricci.

6. Gonzalez, *The Story of Christianity*, 408.

Meeting the Chinese and the Muslims

The cooperative and respectful relationship that was developing between the Church and Chinese culture demonstrates a positive form of both enculturation and interculturation. However, although the blossoming relationship seemed analogous to a good marriage, it was not to last.

THE CHINESE RITES CONTROVERSY

Throughout history many Christians often have been more attached to the outward forms of their religion than to its inner meaning. And, as a result, they feared that if they lost the outward forms they also would lose the inner meaning. Thus, in 1742, many European Catholics, including the priests and bishops, were more attached to the external form of the language of the Latin Mass than to the inner meaning of the breaking of the bread and sharing of the cup. Losing the Latin of the Mass meant losing the Mass itself, or so they feared, and with it the heart of their Catholic religion. This fear persisted in Europe even though the Mass at that time was being celebrated in nine different languages throughout the Catholic world, including the ancient Maronite, Armenian, Chaldean and Greek Melkite rites; and, as recently as 1958, there were 50,000 Maronite Catholics, many in the U.S. and Australia. Most importantly for our subject, these different rites were all local in origin: it was always the local culture that provided the outward form for the different rites of worship.

The Chinese Rites Controversy, which lasted over a century, is so complicated that it's simply impossible to compress even the major issues into a few pages. In 1615, as noted above, Pope Paul V had authorized the use of a Chinese Liturgy. So, for the next 100 years Chinese Rites were celebrated in China. This was a departure from the centuries old Latin European rites, and, in the wake of this, a great controversy ensued between European and Chinese Catholics. By 1742, it was clear that the Pope and the Roman Curia favored the European form of Catholicism. Strangely, Rome did not follow its own instructions issued in 1659: "What could be more absurd than to transplant France, Spain, Italy or some other European country to China?"

But, absurd as it may seem, in 1742, Rome, by papal edict, ended the Chinese Rites Controversy by ruling in favor of the Latin European rites and effectively ending the Chinese mission. In that year, Pope Benedict XIV issued the famous bull *Ex quo singulari*, which stated in part:

> ... we condemn and detest their practice [viz., the Asian rites] as superstitious ... we revoke, annul, abrogate and wish to be deprived of all force and effect, all and each of these permissions, and say and announce that they must be considered for ever to be annulled, null, invalid and without any force or power.[7]

With these brief, but forceful words the creative missionary work of the Jesuits, including that of the saintly Matteo Ricci, effectively came to an end. With the full backing of the Chinese court, the Jesuits did resist the edict, but their efforts had little effect. We can only imagine how different China would be today if the Jesuit mission had been allowed to continue. It would take two hundred years for Rome to change its mind and accept the enculturation policies of Matteo Ricci; this occurred "[i]n 1935 [when] Pope Pius XI approved the cult of Confucius as essentially non-religious, and therefore not opposed to Catholic Doctrine."[8] In 1939, Pope Pius XII went even further and approved the Chinese funeral rites and the cult of the deceased family members. With this decision Rome's attachment to, and idealization of, the European form of Catholicism came to an end, and enculturation of the Chinese culture finally prevailed. But, by this point, it was a little too late.

It would be a mistake, however, to attribute the failure of the Chinese mission, as some Church historians have done, entirely to the Chinese Rites Controversy, or even to Rome's intervention. There were many other powerful dynamics at work within China itself which doomed the mission. Liam Brockey, in his recent book, *Journey to the East: The Jesuit Mission to China, 1579–1724*, exposes a host of other causes for the failure: the missionaries' struggle to learn Chinese with its many local dialects; the over-rapid expansion and too few priests; and, with the short supply of Chinese priests, the responsibility for Church organization fell upon catechists with sanctuaries in their homes, resulting in replacement of the traditional Catholic parish by 'family religion.' In short, the Chinese mission, in the words of one historian, became a "massive house of cards," one that would come tumbling down in the event of a strong wind. And, with the influx of a variety of foreign missionaries, old feuds between religious orders caused divisions in Chinese society. Thus, in 1724, the Chinese emperor officially outlawed the Christian religion.

---

7. Quoted in Johnson, *A History of Christianity*, 414–15.
8. Aylward Shorter, *Toward a Theology of Enculturation*, 159.

Meeting the Chinese and the Muslims

In seeking to determine the primary causes of the failure of the Catholic missions in China, we may see that one of the most significant obstacles to the Jesuit mission and to interculturation was the Chinese language. The Jesuits, coming mostly from Portugal and well educated in Latin, Greek and Hebrew, were quite familiar with the basics of language. But they had never encountered a language as difficult as Chinese. One missionary complained: "... that in fact there was no alphabet, but as many letters as there are words."[9] There were neither articles, nor cases, nor numbers, nor genders, nor tenses, nor modes. Given the complicated structure of the language, "a massive stumbling block was the tonal nature of the spoken language."[10] Words were spelled the same but had a different meaning "with the voice higher or lower in four variations of tone. So, there is little wonder that newly arrived Jesuits had to "spend four years studying the Chinese language and literature."[11] Besides that, many of the older Jesuits had to spend most of their time teaching the Chinese language to new recruits, and could not oversee the work in the missions. Additionally, the Chinese language was also one of the causes for the lack of organization throughout the mission. Basically, the catechists were placed in charge of the operation. There simply were not enough indigenous Chinese priests to oversee the rapid expansion. Liam Brockey, in his conclusions, summarizes much of the language problem:

> Even for the Jesuits, some language barriers remained insurmountable. In those instances, missionaries had to rely on auxiliaries to bridge the gap between a lingua franca and the local dialect—even if this meant sacrificing precision, not to mention the moral problems posed by hearing confessions through intermediaries.[12]

Finally, we need to ask what conclusions we can draw from the Church's mission into the Chinese culture during the sixteenth century that will provide some useful insights for today? We have to conclude that the Jesuit mission was partly successful. First, the Jesuits showed genuine respect for the ancient Chinese culture by an in-depth study of its philosophies and religions. Besides that, they engaged the "new" cul-

---

9. Liam Brockey, *Journey to the East*, 246. Brockey's excellent research relies on the Jesuit archives in Rome and Lisbon, Portugal.
10. Ibid., 247.
11. Ibid.
12. Ibid., 409.

ture in continuous dialogue– a two-way learning process. Second, in the beginning of their mission they related to the Chinese on a humanistic level. They took a positive view of a culture which they did not really understand. Certainly it can be said that God was present to this culture prior to the arrival of the Jesuits. And, even more, the God who became a Jewish human in Jesus was in China as the risen Christ, waiting to be discovered, perhaps in different forms, by all people of faith. The Jesuits respected the Chinese language and so included it in their Eucharistic liturgy and rituals. At the same time, they knew that a culture comprises more than language. For Ricci especially, the Chinese language was only one of many symbols through which one could see and experience the culture. From Ricci's perspective, the language was only one means to an end; it was a door partly open through which one could experience a new world. In short, the Jesuits successfully practiced the Catholic principle of adaptation and accommodation. They embraced the Chinese culture without imposing their own. Through their presence, the historical Jesus, who embraced the Jewish culture yet died for all peoples, in His risen state also embraced the Chinese culture.

There were also many failures, or at least misunderstandings, in the Jesuit mission. European Catholics, and the papacy, did not distinguish the universal faith from its outward European form. They felt that the Latin rite, as practiced uniformly in the European context, was normative shape for the universal Church. Pope Benedict XIV, as well, tended to idealize the European (Latin) form of the faith. In addition to this, there was a great gulf between the papacy and the Curia in Rome, and the missionary workers in the field. Finally, since the Council of Trent (1545–1563), the papacy had been in a defensive, more centralized and over-protective mode. Therefore it failed to distinguish between the discipline of language and unchangeable dogma, between the culture that clothed the faith and the faith itself. So the Chinese language, under these conditions, became a perceived threat to Catholic unity and to the faith itself. In those days many Latin Rite Catholics felt that Latin was a sign of the unity of the Church.

But, of course, this is no longer the case since Vatican II and the multiplication of liturgical languages. Also, since Vatican II, and the *Pastoral Constitution on the Church in the Modern World*, the Church, hopefully, may be less prone to repeat the failures of the past on these counts, though even today it may still learn from them. We perceive in them the importance of native languages, customs and symbols, of indigenous leadership, of church organization, and finally, the important role of the parish in Catholic enculturation. Two cultures, new to each other, cannot 'interculturate' until they learn to communicate clearly and to respect each other as equals. Missionaries need to disengage, at least to some extent, from their home cultures. The experiences of the Chinese missions teach us that real interculturation will be extremely difficult. They also teach us that religion, as in the model of St. Paul, may need to be separated, to some extent, from a specific culture, Roman or Portuguese. Otherwise, it can become an obstacle to true enculturation into a new culture.

THE CHURCH AND MUSLIMS (1095–1291)

In the post 9/11 era, with two wars being fought simultaneously in Afghanistan and Iraq, the television is replete with news and images from the Middle East. Often we are bombarded with scenes of violence and anger, anguish and turmoil, leaving us to wonder about the causes and perhaps our own complicity. Yet, another set of images also has become familiar: streaming pilgrimages to Mecca, the long fasts in Ramadan, faithful Muslims in prayer with long rows of people prostrating in synchronicity all the way to the floor. Yet, although these images are now routine in the West, and are a window into that world, we still do not know much more about the Muslim culture than these common tropes. In the past, especially given the individualistic nature of our own culture, we tended to ignore Muslim culture as something remote and distant from us, even overlooking those of Muslim heritage within our midst. But this is certainly the case no longer; in our multicultural age we have many hard global issues to face:

> Does "war" provide the most appropriate means of adjudicating the conflict between the United States and the Islamic world? Or will war as currently conceived only exacerbate that conflict, rooted in a complex of historically rooted grievances? Is the struggle against Islamic radicalism the latest in a series of American crusades on freedom's behalf? Or does it represent the ugly consequences of previous U. S. policies?[13]

Part of the global issue comes down to sheer numbers: "[t]he current total Muslim population ... is thought to be about 1.3 billion, or roughly one of

---

13. Andrew J. Bacevich, "The Cult of National Security," *Commonweal* CXXXIII, No. 2 (January 27, 2006): 8.

every four or five people alive today. The comparable figure for all branches of Christianity is roughly 1.8 billion people."[14] These numbers alone compel us to become better informed about this growing population.

As Christians in the Pauline tradition, we need to learn how best to interact with this ancient religious culture. We need to find out what are those "historically rooted grievances" noted above. With reflection and prayerful discernment, we can certainly learn a lot through an all-too-brief trip into our mutual history. We may even learn that calling a war "Holy" doesn't make it so. Of necessity we will have to limit our excursion into the complicated Muslim world to a very brief period of that long history. Hopefully, we will get a peek into the Church, into Muslim culture, and, especially, into how the two related, or failed to relate, to each other's religious cultures at that time. The period that will be the most fruitful for discovery and new learning will be the time of the Crusades, or "Holy Wars." But this violent period has a context, and without that we will not reach the deeper understanding needed for determining success or failure in the Church's relationship with Muslim culture. In fact, this is often the case in the instances of those who arrive at the incorrect conclusion that Muslim culture is inherently violent. So, the following section will be divided into two parts: 1) A brief review of the teaching of the Muslim faith, and 2) A brief review of the Crusades or "Holy Wars."

It may be helpful at this point to clarify some terminology. Islam, sometimes called "Muhammadanism," is the religion founded by the prophet, Muhammad (570–632). Muslims (the old spelling was "Moslems") are those who practice Muhammad's Islamic religion. The teachings of Muhammad are contained in three collections: *The Qur'an*, the *Sunna* and the *Hadith*. These collections contain both the sayings and the actions of the prophet. *The Qur'an*, the most important of the three, contains the revelations given by God to Muhammad. Muslims believe the *Qur'an* to be inspired by God, and it is considered to be the 'bible' for the Islamic religion. The book contains 6000 verses arranged in 114 sections. Written in Arabic, the *Qur'an* is about the same length as the Christian New Testament. The *Sunna* is a later collection of Muhammad's deeds and teachings. Another collection of Muhammad's sayings, the *Hadith*, was gathered by his followers two hundred years after his death. Muslim scholars traveled long distances to contact people who had reli-

---

14. Carl W. Ernst, *Following Muhammad*, 59.

able memories. *Jihad*, often used incorrectly to refer to the Muslims' "Holy War," comes from an Arabic word that actually means "to struggle, or to exert oneself." It has a deeply spiritual connotation and can have a wide meaning: for example, "[w]hen some one asked Muhammad what the greatest *jihad* was, the Prophet replied that it was to speak a word of truth in the ear of a tyrant."[15]

Muhammad was born around 570 CE, and, at first, lived with his grandfather, then with his uncle; both of his parents died while he was still young. In 610, when he was forty years old, Muhammad began to receive visions or revelations from God. These revelations increased as the years went on. On the basis of the revelations, Muhammad gathered a group of converts who became his disciples, and the nucleus of the new religion was formed. They traveled, in 622, to the city that would become Medina, known as the "city of the prophet." This pilgrimage marks the beginning of the Islamic religion, and also is the beginning of the Muslim calendar. But, at this time, the Muslims were not well accepted by the people of Mecca and battles ensued off and on until Muhammad's death in 632.

The beliefs of the Muslims are encapsulated in what are called the five pillars of the faith:

1. There is no deity but God, and Muhammad is the messenger of God;
2. There are five regular prayer times each day, facing the Arabian city of Mecca. These are meant to mark off the sacred moments each day from early morning to late evening;
3. Almsgiving. While prayer looks to the individual's spiritual needs, almsgiving looks to the community's external well being...
4. Fasting. This is a rigorous fast during the ninth lunar month of Ramadan.
5. Pilgrimage. All Muslims are expected to make this pilgrimage to Mecca at least once during their lifetime between the eighth and thirteenth days of the twelfth lunar month.[16]

To the five pillars we can add that "Muslims long for a world at peace... Islamic criteria governing the call for a jihad against an outward enemy

---

15. Renard, *Handy Religion Answer Book*, 204.
16. John Renard, *101 Questions on Islam*, 33–34.

Healing and Developing our Multiculturalism

are as stringent as Christianity's terms for waging a 'just war.'"[17] In regard to marriage, the Qur'an does allow polygamy: "... of other women who seem good in your eyes, marry but two, or three, or four; and if ye still fear that ye shall not act equitably, then one only;"[18]

Reading the Qur'an one can easily note the many similarities to the Christian tradition. The five pillars of Islam, noted above, are also pillars for Catholics. Prayer, fasting and almsgiving, for instance, go back to the New Testament. The many pilgrimages to Rome, Lourdes, Fatima, Jerusalem, Tepeyac and Compostela are well to known to most of us. A sacred place can provide a rich spiritual experience.

With its rich and long mystical tradition the Catholic Church is also comfortable with the visions of saints. Beginning with St. Paul's mystical experience, "in the body or out of the body I do not know" (2 Cor 12:2), the Church has celebrated the visions of St. Bernadette of Lourdes, St. Bridget of Sweden, St. John of the Cross, and, recently, St. Juan Diego of Our Lady of Guadalupe, Tepeyac, Mexico. While these visions are not central to the teaching of the Church and often remain regional, nevertheless, they have become part of the church's rich mystical tradition. And, the Catholic Church has never taught that it has a monopoly on mystical experiences, including visions.

In spite of all the above, there have been many tensions between the Muslim culture and the Catholic Church throughout much of their history. During the initial stages of Islam's formation, the Church and Muslim culture enjoyed a very positive, if not warm, relationship: "Primitive Islam had distinguished itself by tolerance... In the conquered regions the Arabs had, for the most part, preserved churches and Christian service. They had not prohibited the practice of Christian charity... Charlemagne sent copious "alms" to Palestine... Pilgrims visited the Holy Land unmolested."[19] However, beginning in 1009, with the Muslim destruction of the Temple of the Resurrection and Golgotha, the relationship was altered drastically. Tensions reached a fever pitch in 1070 when the Turks marched on Palestine and captured Jerusalem. Long before this, Muslims had gradually adopted "the cult of Jerusalem and the holy places. Along with Mecca and Medina, Jerusalem was later recognized as a sacred Muslim city. For

---

17. Ibid., 146.
18. *The Koran*, 45.
19. A. A. Vasiliev, *History of the Byzantine Empire*, II: 391.

the Muhammadans the sacred significance of the city was established by the fact that Muawiya assumed the rank of caliph in Jerusalem."[20] Muslims had actually occupied the Holy Land for four hundred years before Pope Urban II launched the first Crusade in 1095. On account of this, Muslims viewed the 'Holy Wars' as acts of self-defense. The Holy Land, along with Syria, Egypt, North Africa and Spain, was their territory.

European Catholics, who held as sacred their pilgrimages to the Holy Land, would hardly remain passive in the face of Muslim destruction of "their" holy temple in Jerusalem:

> The destruction of the Temple of the Resurrection in 1009 and the conquest of Jerusalem by the Turks in the eighth decade of the eleventh century were facts that profoundly affected the religious-minded masses of Western Europe and evoked a powerful emotion of religious enthusiasm.[21]

Thus, both in the Muslim and in the Catholic cultures, the conditions for war, which set the stage for the First Crusade whose stated aim was 'to recapture the Holy Land,' gradually took shape during the first tentative decades of the eleventh century. But, strange as it may seem, the recapture of the Holy Land may not have been the main reason for the 'Holy Wars'; the real reason may have been more political than 'Holy.' From the letters of Pope Gregory VII, it seems the liberation of the Holy Land was quite secondary:

> Gregory VII was planning an expedition to Constantinople in order to save Byzantium, the chief defender of Christianity in the East. The aid procured by the pope was to be followed by the reunion of the churches and by the return of the schismatic eastern church to the bosom of the "true" catholic church. One is given the impression that in these letters it is a question rather of the protection of Constantinople than of the conquest of the Holy Land.[22]

H. Sybel, a German historian, remarks that another reason for the Crusades "was the growth of the papacy in eleventh century, especially under Gregory VII. Crusades seemed very desirable to the popes, because they opened wide horizons for the further development of the papal power and authority."[23] Gregory VII (1073–1085), who initiated the

---

20. Ibid., I: 217.
21. Ibid., II: 394.
22. Ibid., II: 396.
23. Ibid., II: 397.

much-needed Gregorian Reform, which was named after him, wanted to increase his temporal and spiritual power, especially in Germany, in order to carry out his far-reaching reform program.

Without going further into the many other complicated reasons for the Crusades, we need to briefly review the Crusades themselves. Over a period of two hundred years there were eight major Crusades and a few small additional battles. Pope Urban II in 1095 launched the first Crusade with a rousing speech at the Council of Clermont (in Auvergne, France). The original text of the Pope's speech has been lost, but excerpts like the following have emerged:

> I say it to those who are present. I command that it be said to those who are absent. Christ commands it. All who go thither and lose their lives, be it on the road or on the sea, or in the fight against the pagans, will be granted immediate forgiveness of their sins. This I grant to all who will march, by virtue of the great gift God has given me.[24]

Only one Crusade succeeded in gaining control over the Holy Land, Western possession of which lasted only for a period of fifteen years. In terms of sheer devastation and loss of life, the fourth Crusade (1203) was by far the worst. Karen Armstrong gives us some of the gory details:

> The sack of Constantinople was one of the great crimes of history. For three days the Venetians and Crusaders rushed through the streets, raping, killing and pillaging with a horrible eagerness. Women and children lay dying in the streets and nuns were raped in their convents ... never since the history of the creation of the world had so much booty been taken from a city: no one could possibly count the piles of gold, silver and jewels or the bales of precious materials.[25]

So what can we learn from the failures of the Crusades to help us dialogue, interact and build bridges with the Muslims of today? The importance of the Crusades for Catholic/Muslim relations can hardly be overestimated. Karen Armstrong, a noted historian, writes:

> In *Holy War* I tried to show that the Crusades were not a fringe movement in the Middle Ages; they were central to the new Western identity that was forged at this time and which persists

24. Gonzalez, *The Story of Christianity*, 292.
25. Armstrong, *Holy War*, 386.

Meeting the Chinese and the Muslims

to the present day... Pope Urban II called the First Crusade in 1095, but the hatred and suspicion that this expedition unleashed still reverberates, never more so than on September 11, 2001, and during the terrible days that followed."[26]

At the outset we note that there were more failures than successes. First, we did not engage the Muslims in dialogue about their faith. The enmity that grew between Muslims and the Catholic Church was more about earthly power than about faith. Second, it should be clear from foregoing that today the burden of initiating a process of reconciliation falls squarely on us. The first step needs to be a sincere confession of "our fault, our fault, and our most grievous fault." We can pray along with the *Decree on Ecumenism* from Vatican II: "... in humble prayer, we beg pardon of God and of our separated brethren (Muslims), just as we forgive those who trespass against us."[27] Third, in spite of the media and their unfair tendency to stereotype and highlight extremes, we need to learn to think more positively about Muslim culture. Thus, we ought to offer the kiss of peace and live in peace with all Muslims. Fourth, we must sit down with Muslim sisters and brothers and discuss those beliefs which we have in common. With six million Muslims in the U.S. that should not be hard to do. Finally, we can pray with them a beautiful prayer from the *Qur'an* (Sura 87):

> Praise the name of the Lord most high,
> Who hath created and balanced all things,
> Who hath fixed their destinies and guideth them,
> Who bringeth forth the pasture?
> And reduceth it to dusty stubble...
> Happy he who is purified by Islam,
> And who remembereth the name of the Lord and prayeth.
> But ye prefer this present life,
> Though the life to come is better and more enduring.[28]

Briefly reviewing just two cultures is hardly enough to form a good pastoral judgment about how to interact with today's explosive intersection of cultures. So, in the next chapter, we will review two other cultures which may provide deeper insights for today's challenge of multiculturalism.

---

26. Armstrong, *Holy War*, ix. Karen Armstrong's well-researched book will probably become a classic on this subject.

27. DVII, No. 7.

28. *The Koran*, 398.

QUESTIONS FOR DISCUSSION

1. If you were having breakfast at McDonald's with two recent arrivals from China, what would you discuss first?
2. List the three qualities in the Chinese culture that you would like to import into our culture.
3. What parts of the U.S. culture will be the hardest for the Chinese to accept?
4. How do you feel when you see the Muslims bowing down to the floor in prayer?
5. What surprised you the most about the Crusades?
6. In terms of feelings, what is the most difficult in initiating a dialogue with Muslims?
7. Do you get the feeling that your Muslim friend is angry at the U.S.? Why?

3

Meeting the Latinos and the Jews

As noted in the last chapter, selecting three or four cultures out of the many in the U.S. is fairly arbitrary. Here, however, we are more interested in what we can learn from the Church's encounter with different cultures than with making a complete survey of all the specific cultures themselves. Pastoral theology grows both from above—through new insights into God's revelation, and from below—through the incarnation of the Word in specific earthly cultures. But often it is the specific cultural incarnation, like Jesus in Jewish flesh, which reveals the deepest meaning of the truths that come "from above." And this deeper meaning is the new understanding we seek both from the successes and failures in our Church's encounters with the Latino and Jewish cultures.

OUR CHURCH AND THE LATINO CULTURES

With eleven million undocumented immigrants scattered throughout the U.S., it's extremely difficult to measure the Church's success or failure with today's variety of cultures. Today, in the U.S., the Latino culture, by sheer numbers, is the largest ethnic minority group. Given this, we will concentrate our examination on the Latino cultures since they constitute the present face of our multicultural reality. The Church's response, for good or for ill, varies considerably from diocese to diocese. Within the many books on the issue of immigration, and the fusion or osmosis of the Latino cultures within the U.S., it appears that either U.S. culture may be in the process of being assimilated into the Latino cultures, or the whole U.S. culture, willy-nilly, is being shaped into islands of many distinct enclaves of different cultures. Perhaps the most controversial, and, at the same time, most insightful, work is *Mexifornia* by professor Victor Davis Hanson of California State University. Hanson is well connected with the grassroots of the Latino "invasion" of California, and states the dilemma facing the U.S. in clear, unambiguous terms. His conclusions are not limited to California but, as he argues in the appropriately titled final chapter, "The Fork in the Road," will apply to the whole U.S.

Eventually—the sooner, the better—all the churches, all the immigrants, and all levels of the U.S. government will have to face the following dilemma: separatism or assimilation? The decision is unavoidable, though we may choose to ignore or act obliviously toward it. However, as Richard Lamm, the former governor of Colorado, warns that inaction may lead to the self-destruction of both our culture and our country. As Church, we are a moving pilgrimage. If we do nothing, we may find our pilgrimage on the wrong road by default. The fork approaches, not just the Church or the government, but *all people*, including the immigrants, who now live in these multicultural United States.

Since most of our Latino/a immigrants come from Mexico, a little history of Mexico may help us gain perspective. In 1519 Hernan Cortés, one of several Spanish conquistadores, landed on the island of Cozumel, Mexico. With him were 550 Europeans, hundreds of slaves, five priests, some attack dogs and some small cannon.[1] While there had been other conquistadores who had led expeditions to this "new" world, the persistent and aggressive Cortés was the most successful in actually conquering the native inhabitants. Through him and his army all of Mexico was eventually subjugated to the Spanish Royal Crown, and the conquered land renamed "New Spain." One of the many reasons claimed for the expedition by Cortés was to convert the natives to the Catholic Faith. Yet it is clear that most of the conquistadores were looking for gold; others simply wanted to exploit the resources of the new land, and even the native population. Gold, silver, and precious stones, feathers, mantles, embroidered goods and Indian slaves, both men and women, were readily available in the marketplace.[2]

Since the conquistadores had set sail for the East Indies, they incorrectly called the natives of this new land 'Indians;' but little did they know at that time that some of these 'Indians,' like the Olmecs, represented an ancient culture dating back to 1200 BCE. While Cortés smashed idols, the priests who accompanied him seemed to be content with the Indian

---

1. Foster, *A Brief History of Mexico*, 48.
2. Ibid., 9.

customs, so long as they did not offer human sacrifices. In keeping with the Spanish tradition of the union of Church and State, the emperor of Spain, Charles V, following the recommendation of Cortés, appointed the Franciscans, Dominicans and Augustinians to take charge of the mission to the Mexican Indians; and by 1537 nine million natives had been baptized.[3] According to one priest:

> It was not unusual to baptize 4000 converts in a day . . . Most anthropologists believe the Virgin (of Guadalupe) represents a powerful synthesis of the Christian and Mesoamerican beliefs: she is still called Tonantzin by the Nahua. Many such instances of a syncretic religion have been identified, including the performance of Ch'a-Chek rituals to the Maya rain god.[4]

Spain controlled the conquered land down to the smallest details, imposing its own social caste system. For almost 300 years Spain, with blood curdling cruelty, ruled Mexico, imposing its language, culture and religion on the native 'Indians.' The conquistadores retained control by reducing most of the native population to slavery through the inhumane *encomienda* system.[5] However, the tight grip of the Spanish conquistadores would not last.

On September 16, 1810, standing on the church steps in the city of Dolores, Fr. Miguel Hidalgo rallied his parishioners around a banner of Our Lady of Guadalupe to march in protest to Spanish rule. Thousands more soon joined the march: so began the Mexican War for Independence. After the brutal killing and decapitation of Fr. Hidalgo, his protégé, Fr. Jose Moreles gathered an army from a variety of classes throughout Mexico. All his soldiers wore the badge of Our Lady of Guadalupe. With this nondescript, but highly motivated, army Moreles continued the war. On September 27, 1821, under the leadership of Augustin de Iturbide, the Plan of Córdoba was signed with Spain. The plan proposed a constitutional monarchy for Mexico. With the signing of this plan the eleven-year War of Independence concluded, and Mexico was finally free from the cruel yoke of Spanish rule.

The end of Spanish rule, however, did not bring peace. For the next twenty-five years Mexico suffered under the chaotic regimes of Iturbide

---

3. Ibid., 66.
4. Ibid., 69
5. See Paul S. Vickery, *Bartolome de las Casas*, 125–26.

and General Santa Anna. And, on May 9, 1846, U.S. President James Polk went to Congress to get a declaration of war with Mexico. Polk claimed Mexico had invaded U.S. territory when Mexican soldiers killed sixteen U.S. soldiers on disputed territory in Texas. Soon after the declaration of war, U.S. General Winfield Scott's army landed at Veracruz. By August, 1847, General Scott had conquered Mexico City. On February 2, 1848, the U.S. and Mexico signed the treaty of Guadalupe Hidalgo through which the U.S. annexed a large portion of northern Mexico. Today that land includes all of California, Arizona, New Mexico, Nevada, Texas, Utah, and half of Colorado. Except for the Gadsden Purchase in 1853, these two years of war, "initiated" by the U.S., shaped the geography of the U.S. and Mexico more than any other event to the present day.

But all of this did not end warfare in Mexico. In 1858, the French invaded Mexico, landing at Veracruz. Six thousand five hundred French troops then marched on to Puebla. However, four years later, on May 5, 1862, the Mexican army expelled the French army from Puebla. This great victory is still celebrated as the holiday *Cinco de Mayo*. But a period of immense chaos followed the declaration of independence and the adoption of a constitution. Mexico became a country polarized between the Church and the government. A wave of anti-clericalism, both in the new reform laws and in the confused culture, gained momentum.

The Reform Laws passed by Benito Juarez:

> ... clearly made the church subservient to the state. All church properties had been confiscated. Monasteries were closed. Public religious displays were curtailed. ... Juarez decreed that religious were forbidden to wear their vestments in public and threatened imprisonment to any priest fostering disrespect for the government and its laws.[6]

Only recently have these anti-clerical laws been repealed.

Much of the tumultuous history of Mexico can be summed up, though too simply, by wars, oil, bribes, chaos, migration, poverty, corruption, discrimination, the military interference of foreign powers, strong family bonds, and, finally, genuine devotion to Our Lady of Guadalupe. But even more, there are no words in any language that can describe adequately the bloody genocide the Spanish inflicted on the poor, innocent Latinos for three hundred years. That the natives even survived so much

---

6. Foster, 132.

unjust suffering is a miracle of grace. It is inspiring to hear them sing with gusto during their Sunday Liturgies: "A free people walking through the waters of life."[7] They have also walked through fire, and they have risen to new life. Purified by their many trials, the Mexican immigrants may indeed renew the U.S. Church.

THE ESCAPE FROM POVERTY AND STARVATION

The current cultural situation in the U.S. is one in which there is a visible and plentiful presence of Latino/as, yet it is difficult to know precisely the extent of their presence given the inaccuracy of numbers and records on account of undocumented migration. The variability can be seen in conflicting reports on undocumented immigration, where "[e]stimates vary from fewer than 100,000 to more than 500,000 each year."[8] However, the phenomenon of undocumented migration is not entirely new, as Chavez reports, "since 1980 about two million Latino immigrants have come to the United States legally."[9] In light of this, we ask why they come, whether through legal immigration channels or as undocumented? The answer is fairly simple: in 2007 *fifty two million* Mexicans were found to be living below the poverty line. Even more, in the region of Chiapas alone *70% of the people live in abject poverty*. So, then, the answer to the query of why they are here, and why they risk their lives to come is obvious; they come to get jobs, to feed their families, and to find a better life in the "paradise" on the other side of the U.S. border. And they will continue to do so—fence or no fence, law or no law. The crying need to escape their cruel poverty overrides everything. We can be certain that St. Thomas Aquinas' moral theology would certainly bless the Latinos for breaking a mere human law to save their own lives from death-dealing hunger.[10] And we should not forget that we have a holiday dedicated to Dr. Martin Luther King who became a hero for breaking our racist laws.

So how should the churches respond to the influx of new Latinos and Latinas, legal or undocumented? Must we support the government in building a seven hundred mile fence along the U.S.-Mexican border?

---

7. "Pueblo Libre," in *Flor y Canto*, no. 384.
8. Chavez, *Out of the Barrio*, 122.
9. Ibid.
10. See, for instance, Aquinas, *Summa Theologica*, IIaIIae.Q59.a2-4; Q66.a5-8.

Or, ought we to build houses of hospitality all along the border with signs like:

> "The Christian Churches welcome you.
> Help yourselves to the water."

Perhaps we could install a thousand small replicas of the Statue of Liberty, with those ancient but still sacred lines:

> Give me your tired, your poor,
> Your huddled masses yearning to breathe free,
> The wretched refuse of your teeming shore.
> Send these, the homeless tempest-tossed to me.
> I lift my lamp beside the golden door.[11]

The Catholic Church gave a provisional response to this situation, when, in 2003, the bishops of the U.S. and Mexico collaborated in publishing an extremely important document entitled, *Strangers no Longer: Together on the Journey of Hope*. In this document, the Bishops defend the Latinos' right to migrate:

> Catholic teaching has a long and rich tradition in defending the right to migrate. Based on the life and teachings of Jesus, the Church's teaching has provided the basis for the development of basic principles regarding the right to migrate for those attempting to exercise their *God-given human rights*. Catholic teaching also states that the root causes of migration–poverty, injustice, religious intolerance, armed conflict–must be addressed so that migrants can remain in their homeland and support their families.[12]

U.S. and Mexican bishops, as is clear from the above, envision a cooperative effort between the Church and the governments of both countries. It is important to note the affirmation of this document that the right to migrate is a *"God-given human right."* Migratory rights are not conferred by courts, governments, or human laws; nor are they dependent on color, race, religion, ethnic origin or economic status. "Regardless of their legal status," the bishops proclaim, "migrants, like all human persons, possess inherent human dignity that should be respected."[13] However, in a note of criticism,

---

11. Emma Lazarus, "The New Colossus," in *The Poems of Emma Lazarus* (New York: MacMillan, 2007), 1: 172.

12. United States Conference of Catholic Bishops, *Strangers no Longer*, 13. [Italics mine].

13. Ibid., 16.

the document states that "Mexican enforcement of immigration laws... has been marked by corruption, police brutality, and systemic abuses of basic human rights. Migrants are often forced to bribe Mexican police to continue transit and, if unable to produce payments, are beaten and returned to the border."[14]

The Church, and, indeed, we all are under obligation to translate the bishops' words into action on both sides of the border. This is the more difficult challenge, but the bishops have some helpful recommendations: "Making legal the large number of undocumented workers from many nations who are in the United States would help to stabilize the labor market in the United States, to preserve family unity, and so improve the standard of living in immigrant communities."[15] In order to humanize the situation, the present complicated legalization process needs to be simplified. By eliminating 50% of the present bureaucracy and restrictions, the waiting period could be reduced from today's ten years to three years in most cases. The multiplication and complexification of laws reflects our own culture's pathology of fear and paranoia since the tragedy of 9/11. That pathology is often exploited by self-serving, political rhetoric. There is a stark and visible difference between the poor Latinos and Latinas, seeking jobs and escape from hunger, and terrorist operatives seeking to cause further damage and destruction to the U.S. after 9/11; and, there is no mistaking the two, though the network of U.S. laws refuses, or ignores, any such distinction. Our over-extended military and the multiplication of regulations without end are more the result of media-inspired fear than the threats of a real enemy.

It may be helpful to note that by 1837 the U.S. Congress had granted limited amnesty thirty-nine times to the hundreds of thousands of squatters who disregarded the law and occupied federal lands. Twenty-five years later, "the 1862 Homestead Act granted free title to settlers who met the statute's five year residency and improvement requirements."[16] The squatters were then called "settlers" and finally, "pioneers." So, "much of the territory of the U.S. was," in fact, *settled by illegal squatters.*"[17]

---

14. Ibid., 40.

15. Ibid.

16. Eduardo Moisés Peñalver, "Are the Illegal Immigrants Pioneers? *Commonweal* 133 (2006): 9.

17. Ibid. (Italics mine).

The present immigration system, scandalously, may be indirectly responsible for the deaths of over two thousand migrants trying to cross into the United States between 1998 and 2002. The causes of these migrants' death range from heat strokes, dehydration, hypothermia, and drowning.[18] Surely, as a rich, civilized Christian country, we can and must do better. At a minimum, we could follow the example of Tucson's "Humane Borders" and set up water stations along the border from San Diego to Brownsville, TX. Then, after the immigration system has been thoroughly reformed and more humane laws have been passed, we could expand these stations into "Houses of Hospitality." We could add essential equipment like maps, food, medicines, etc. After a brief, but careful, screening process, we could help the migrants find jobs and even help them get started on the road to U.S. citizenship.

The U.S. and Mexican bishops also recommend that "the U.S. employment-based immigration system should be reformed to feature both *permanent* and, with appropriate protections, *temporary* visa programs for laborers."[19] After all, the migrants come to get jobs to feed their families. If, at the end of their visas, they decide to settle in a specific area of the U.S., they will also be faced with the fork in the road: Separatism or assimilation; or, even, a combination of the two.[20]

All of the above does *not* imply a policy of open borders. Terrorists do exist, and they would certainly exploit such a naïve and unreal 'solution' as entirely open and unregulated borders. And, just as cities cannot survive without a police force, likewise no country can long remain secure without some kind of enforced border patrol. The kingdom of God has not arrived yet, and so we cannot expect infallibility in plans and structures, or in those who enter into our space. Without falling victim to paranoia and fear, the U.S. has enough enemies to be wary of a total vacancy at its borders.

Now, to return to the fork in the road. There is no doubt that the churches, and the whole U.S., must soon decide between separatism and assimilation. Separatism is a denial of *E Pluribus Unum*, the motto inscribed at the founding of the country. For Latinos, separatism involves, within their communities, a "profound distrust of non-Hispanic and ma-

---

18. Ibid., 42.
19. Ibid., 36.
20. For more details, see Hanson, *Mexifornia,* 142–150.

jority institutions." At least four Latino/a groups, including La Raza, have tried to organize around a separatist approach:

> According to the leaders of these groups, Anglo society would never accept Mexican Americans as full and equal participants, no matter how hard Mexican Americans tried to conform to the values of the majority culture. Therefore, they argued, Mexican Americans must separate themselves from the majority society.[21]

Another aspect of separatism is the tendency for some Latinos and Latinas to cling tenaciously to their native culture, and refuse to participate in the customs and political process of their adopted country. This dynamic includes the formation of social ghettoes within the Latino/a communities: Latino/a business owners and operators hire only other Latino/as; friendships and socializing are restricted to fellow Latinos and Latinas. Part of the equation—and only partially—is a language problem. That it involves more than language can be seen in the fact that many bi-lingual Latino/as are hesitant to place their full trust in their fellow U.S. citizens (for instance, many do not trust a white babysitter). Unconsciously, perhaps, they are pressured to choose the road to separatism.

Those who live in Latino/a ghettoes are also on the road to separatism. Often it is their poverty which draws them together into a poor mobile home park. Through no fault of their own, they end up in the poor section of the city. Sometimes their own strong family bonds keep them isolated from the rest of the population. Separatism is the easier road in the cultural fork, all the more so when the "welcoming" culture does nothing.

But separatism will lead to self-destruction. No culture or civilization can survive when it is divided into hundreds of separate cultural islands. In fact, the built-in tensions, as history teaches us, will lead to wars, crime, and violence. All societies and civilizations require unifying structures. A common religion could be one unifying bond across diverse cultures. But so far, a bond that really works, has not been found. In our individualistic society, the all-too-human tendency toward polarization seems to be stronger than all the unifying bonds of religion, culture and human laws.

The alternative prong to separatism is the old-but-reliable dynamic of assimilation. Assimilation into the common fabric of American society

---

21. Chavez, *Out of the Barrio*, 68–69.

was the normative pattern of the great immigrations of Irish, German, Italians. Certainly we are capable of instituting immigration reform which respects the human dignity of today's immigrants so they will feel equal to our earlier immigrants. This kind of reform will welcome the immigrant Latinos with their own hallowed maxim: *Mi casa es su casa*. Assimilation is the more difficult road, but the Church, with its manifold experiences of failures and successes, can be a vital resource. The life, message, and experiences of the Church are a rich treasure now available to all of the many cultures dwelling in the U.S.

However, in order for the Church to be openly accessible, the Church must first confess its mistakes, its sins of discrimination and persecution of the Mexican immigrants. Bishop Patricio Flores, in a speech given in Washington, DC, in June, 1972, tells us why a confession of sins is necessary as a prelude to assimilation:

> From us have been stolen our lands, our language, our culture, our customs, our history and our way of religious expression. We have also been victims of oppression, discrimination, semi-slavery. We have been poorly paid for our work; we have lived in housing worse than that of monkeys in a zoo; we have not been admitted to some schools.[22]

In confessing its own sins, the Church needs to take the lead in a process of reconciliation. Only then will the Church become credible in the task of supporting assimilation. Additionally, the Church needs to show compassion for the immigrants' inner, emotional struggle in leaving their homeland and adopting a new way of life in a multicultural country. Such adjustments are never easy, especially in the face of grinding poverty and subtle forms of discrimination. Jorge Ramos describes the emotional ups and downs of his own personal journey in his book, *No Borders*:

> There exists, without a doubt, a point of no return, and that is when our lives in our new country are more intense than the memories nourished by nostalgia. Finally, the accumulation of experiences abroad causes our memories to lose the importance they once had when we first left, and they become yet another chapter of an odyssey.[23]

---

22. Quoted in Sandoval, *On the Move*, 100.
23. Ramos, *No Borders*, 298–99.

Meeting the Latinos and the Jews

THE CHURCH AND THE JEWS

I remember well the old tradition where, on Good Friday, the priest celebrating the Liturgy, among a list of other prayers, prayed for the "perfidious Jews." And in accordance with the affirmational response, along with everybody else in church, I said "Amen." It was many years later that I learned that the Latin, *perfidia*, meant faithless, not treacherous. But that did not do much for my state of shock at hearing such language. After all, even as a youngster, I knew that Jewish folks went to the synagogues and believed in the same God that we did. How could our Church publicly call them faithless? This pronunciation was repeated every year in the Holy Week liturgy prior to Vatican II. For those unfamiliar with, or too young to have experienced the pre-revised Liturgy, and the oldsters who have forgotten, this shocking Good Friday prayer runs as follows:

> "Almighty and eternal God, who drivest not away from thy mercy even the faithless Jews (Latin: *Judaicam perfidiam*), hear our prayers, which we offer for the blindness of that people . . . that they may be delivered from their darkness."[24]

Even before the reforms of Vatican II, Pope John XXIII, in 1959, ordered the Latin phrase, *Judaicam perfidiam*, removed from the Good Friday liturgy. Since Vatican II, the whole prayer has been removed and replaced with a new prayer. Now we pray: ". . . that the people you first made your own may arrive at the fullness of redemption." And, on February 5, 2008, the Good Friday prayer was changed once again, this time by Pope Benedict XVI, to read:

> Let us also pray for the Jews. May the Lord our God enlighten their hearts so that they may acknowledge Jesus Christ, the savior or all men. All powerful and everlasting God, you who want men to be saved and to reach the awareness of the truth, graciously grant that with the fullness of peoples entering your church, all of Israel may be saved. Through Christ, our Lord. Amen."

Understandably, many Jews and Catholics feel this new prayer represents a step backwards from the progress in friendly relations that has been made over the last 40 years. According to these advocates against the newest revisions, the prayer is a call to convert the Jews to Christianity.

---

24. Fiedler and Rabben, eds., *Rome Has Spoken*, 72.

Healing and Developing our Multiculturalism

But, fortunately, many groups, both Jewish and Catholic, have determined to continue their fruitful dialogues.

That our Catholic Church over the centuries has been guilty of anti-Semitism is hardly news. But, a brief review of a few of the worst periods in history may shed some light on why the ecumenical task ahead of us may be difficult. Anti-Semitism goes back all the way to the Church's early Patristic period. St. John Chrysostom (c. 400) wrote that "the synagogue is a bordello,... a hiding place for unclean beasts."[25] And, Origen (230) gives us a "theological" reason for the Church's anti-Semitism: "And therefore the blood of Jesus falls not only on the Jews of that time, *but on all generations of Jews up to the end of the world.*"[26] Many Christians believed, alongside Origen, that the Jews, as a race, were guilty of crucifying Jesus Christ, i.e. deicide. According to this viewpoint, it is acknowledged that the Roman soldiers performed the actual execution, but the Jews insisted upon it when, answering Pilate, they cried out: "Crucify Him!" (Mk 15:13); this position, even more, reads quite literally the claim of culpability in St. Matthew's Gospel (Mt 27: 24-26). Thus, the guilt of a few was believed to extend to a whole people. Essentially the whole Church, for centuries, accepted Origen's flawed rationale in one form or another. The whole Jewish race, it was believed, became eternally guilty, and so *any* Jewish person was held to be culpable just because he or she was born Jewish. The theology of Origen, hereby, provided a religious grounding for anti-Semitism.

During the Crusades, as noted in the previous chapter, the crusaders, in their religious hatred, often did not distinguish between Jews and Muslims: "the mobs (crusaders), in 1096, turned to outright massacre—twelve Jews were murdered at Speier, five hundred at Worms, one thousand at Mainz, twenty-two at Metz, and so forth."[27] There is also considerable evidence that the Church was complicit in the formation of Jewish ghettoes. In 1434, the Council of Basil decreed:

> (Jews) are to be forced under threat of heavy penalties to take on a form of dress by which they can be clearly distinguished from Christians. Moreover, in order to avoid excessive social intercourse, they must be made to dwell separate from Christians in their cities and towns, in places as far distant from the churches as possible.

---

25. Ibid., 67.
26. Ibid. [Italics mine].
27. Johnson, *A History of Christianity*, 245.

Meeting the Latinos and the Jews

Nor may they on Sundays and other solemn feast days open their shops or work in public.[28]

The formation of ghettoes, of course, is the exact opposite of St. Paul's command: "be generous in offering hospitality" (Rom 13:13). It is also a contradiction of the hospitality the Jewish people themselves had practiced since the law of Leviticus: "You shall treat the alien who resides with you no differently than the natives born among you; have the same love for him as for yourself" (Lev 19:34).

We do not have space to discuss the very complicated problems of the German Jews under Hitler's reign, and Pope Pius XII's controversial response, or non-response, to the terrible persecution of the Jews during World War II (1938-45). Suffice it to say, that the churches, often by silence, permitted Hitler's persecution to proceed without much opposition—all the way to the horrors of the Holocaust. Not all German Catholics, however, were merely passive observers. We know that 22.7 per cent of Hitler's S.S. troops were practicing Catholics.[29] And, they were quite active in the terrible murders of the Holocaust. No doubt their anti-Semitic prejudice was stronger and deeper than their Catholicism. We look in vain for a prophetic Catholic voice, like Dietrich Bonhoeffer, who condemned the war and the "mindless Christian patriotism" which spread across Germany like a national disease.

This anti-Semitic pathology was so deeply rooted in the German national psyche that Hitler could carry out perhaps the greatest crime of genocide in history. He was able to do this because the whole German culture was infected with anti-Semitism. We have to admit and confess to God, and to our fellow Jewish neighbors, that the Catholic and Protestant churches were complicit in developing an anti-Semitic German culture in which a Hitler, with the cooperation of his troops, could commit some of the most horrible crimes of history.

The Third Reich's teaching that the Germans were a superior race contributed strongly to the culture's anti-Semitism. But, the Catholic Church had enacted a body of anti-Jewish laws going back at least to the regional Council of Elvira (304), which decreed: "If, indeed, some one of the clergy or faithful has taken a meal with Jews, it is determined that as a corrective punishment he is to abstain from communion" (Canon

---

28. Fiedler and Rabben, *Rome has Spoken*, 70.
29. Johnson, *A History of Christianity*, 491.

50).³⁰ The Fourth Lateran Council (1215), an ecumenical council, forbade intermarriage with Jews, and decreed, further, that Jews be required to wear "special clothing and a badge."³¹ Hitler's thoroughly evil Nuremberg Laws, passed by parliament in 1935, were worse than the Church laws, but shared a common sentiment. The Nuremberg laws "segregated the Jews, [and] made them ineligible for employment and ultimately deprived them of human rights."³² The German anti-Semitic culture, nourished by both Church and state, was ready to accept such scandalous, inhumane laws.

We can hardly omit the influence of the anti-Semitic *Protocols of the Elders of Zion*. Published in 1903, and translated into many languages, it fueled the myth that the Jews were a subversive political underground with a plan for world domination. Even though it was soon proven to be a malicious forgery, it remained a powerful contributor to anti-Semitic sentiment throughout Europe and beyond. Jews were blamed for the Bolshevik Revolution on the basis of the book's thesis. The *Protocols*, even after it was known to be a forgery, was published and republished by a wide variety of anti-Semitic organizations in Europe and in the U.S.; even Wal-Mart sold the book on its website for a time. Today, in the U.S., the *Protocols* is distributed by Louis Farrakhan's Nation of Islam.

God's call to repentance, conversion, penance, and reconciliation rings in our ears day and night. Too late do we weep for our brothers and sisters who gave the world the abundant riches of the Jewish tradition. However, we are trying hard to make amends to our Jewish sisters and brothers living today.

PENITENCE AND CONVERSION

John XXIII was elected pope in 1958, and, in spite of his advanced age, he did not wait long to announce his program of *aggiornamento* (a bringing up to date). He "opened a window," and, to the surprise of the Catholic world, convoked the Second Vatican Council on October 11, 1962. Surrounded by those in the Roman Curia who were less enthusiastic for the new Council, he prayed that the Holy Spirit " renew his wonders in our time, as though for a new Pentecost."³³One of the many great fruits

---

30. Jurgens, *The Faith of the Early Fathers*, 256.
31. Mary C. Boys, ed. *Seeing Judaism Anew*, 7.
32. Ibid.
33. "Pope John Convokes the Council," in DVII, 709.

of that "new Pentecost" was a radical conversion regarding the traditional Catholic attitude toward the Jews. On October 28, 1965, the Council approved the *Declaration on the Relationship of the Church to Non-Christian Religions* (*Nostra Aetate*). It included a fairly large section (No. 4) on the Church's relations with the Jewish people. *The Declaration* passed easily by a vote of 2,221 to 88.

From the viewpoint of Catholic theology, and the painful history of the Church's anti-Semitism, the following section of that *Declaration* is a clear sign of the Church's change of heart:

> True, the authorities of the Jews and those who followed their lead pressed for the death of Christ (cf. Jn 19:6); still, what happened in His passion cannot be blamed upon all the Jews then living, without distinction, nor upon the Jews of today. Although the Church is the new people of God, the Jews should not be presented as repudiated or cursed by God, as if such views followed from the holy Scriptures ... The Church repudiates all persecutions against any man. Moreover, mindful of her common patrimony with the Jews, and motivated by the gospel's spiritual love, and by no political considerations, she deplores the hatred, persecutions, and displays of anti-Semitism directed against the Jews at any time and from any source.[34]

This section of the *Declaration* deals directly and clearly with the historical and erroneous extension of the guilt of the "authorities of the Jews" of that time to other Jews, and to the Jews of today. Fortunately, these powerful words of conversion have not remained just a dead letter in a conciliar text.

The late Pope John Paul II, in 1990, speaking primarily of the Holocaust, repudiated all persecution of the Jews: "For Christians, the heavy burden of guilt for the murder of the Jewish people must be an enduring call to repentance; thereby we can overcome every form of anti-Semitism and establish a new relationship with our kindred nation of the Old Covenant."[35] These words were a public confession in the name of our Church. We can only hope and pray that our Jewish brothers and sisters will absolve us from our sin of anti-Semitism and help us begin that "new relationship."

---

34. DVII, No. 4.
35. Fiedler and Rabben, Eds. *Rome Has Spoken*, 73.

Healing and Developing our Multiculturalism

Our late pope certainly gave us some exemplary leadership: 1) in 1986, he visited the synagogue in Rome, becoming the first pope to do so; 2) in 1994, he established full diplomatic relations with Israel; and, 3) in March 2000, he prayed for Israel's forgiveness at the Wailing Wall in Jerusalem. He placed a petition in one of the cracks in the Western Wall; the text of his prayer reads:

> God of our fathers, you chose Abraham and his descendants to bring your Name to the Nations. We are deeply saddened by the behavior of those who in the course of history have caused these children of yours to suffer, and asking your forgiveness we wish to commit ourselves to genuine brotherhood with the people of the Covenant.[36]

Fr. John Pawlikowski, following the pope's example, reminds us that according to Paul's letter to the Romans "…the covenant of the Jews remains intact even after Jesus' death (Rom 9–11)."

Fr. Pawlikowski continues:

> There is no basis for the indictment of the Jews as the killers of Jesus. Jews are still an integral part of the covenant with God initiated on Mt. Sinai. Jesus and his church were fundamentally impacted by Judaism. Jesus was fully integrated into the Jewish tradition of his time.[37]

On September 1, 2002, a truly historic document was published by the Christian Scholars Group on Christian-Jewish Relations; entitled, "A Sacred Obligation," it includes these ten principles:

1. God's covenant with the Jewish people endures forever.
2. Jesus of Nazareth lived and died as a faithful Jew.
3. Ancient rivalries must not define Christian-Jewish relations today.
4. Judaism is a living faith, enriched by many centuries of development.
5. The Bible both connects and separates Jews and Christians.
6. Affirming God's enduring covenant with the Jewish people has consequences for Christian understandings of salvation.
7. Christians should not target Jews for conversion.

---

36. Quoted by Eugene Fisher in *Seeing Judaism Anew*, 261.
37. Pawlikowski, *Tower Topics,* XX, No. 1 (Spring, 2006), 17.

8. Christian worship that teaches contempt for Judaism dishonors God.
9. We affirm the importance of the land of Israel for the life of the Jewish people.
10. Christians should work with Jews for the healing of the world.[38]

These principles can be considered a manifesto to be proclaimed by all Christians to everyone, anywhere in the world. But, they are only the beginning of a new era in relations between Jews and Christians. The manifesto must still pass from the world of the scholars to the workaday world of the rest of us. Catholics could start by a prayerful study of the Hebrew Bible, a new understanding of what the Catholic faith and tradition shares in common with the Jewish faith.

All of the churches need to engage our multicultural context—Jewish, Chinese, Muslim and Latino/a, etc.—in a meaningful dialogue. Diocesan and parish pastoral councils could set up a standing interfaith committee on multiculturalism, in which such a committee would be both a witness to our change of heart and, at the same time, a call to concrete actions. Real dialogue with Jewish communities could be the first of these concrete gestures. Such dialogue should include the four forms of dialogue recommended by the Pontifical Council for Interreligious Dialogue and the Congregation of Peoples:

a) *The dialogue of life,* where people strive to live in an open and neighborly spirit, sharing their joys and sorrows, their human problems and preoccupations.

b) *The dialogue of action,* which Christians and others collaborate for the integral development and liberation of people.

c) *The dialogue of theological exchange,* where specialists seek to deepen their understanding of their respective religious heritages, and to appreciate each other's spiritual values.

d) *The dialogue of religious experience,* where persons, rooted in their own religious traditions, share their spiritual riches, for instance, with regard to prayer and contemplation, faith and ways of searching for God or the Absolute.[39]

---

38. Boys, *Seeing Judaism Anew,* xiv-xvii.

39. Pontifical Council for Interreligious Dialogue and the Congregations of Peoples, *Dialogue and Proclamation,* (Rome: 1991), 42.

This kind of dialogue will be rich in increasing mutual understanding, and, at the same time, it will deepen the faith of the partners to the dialogue.

So what have we learned from our reflections on the Church and the Jewish and Latino/a cultures? First, the Church, as a living, sinful body is vulnerable to all the "-isms" in any given culture. The Church, of necessity enfleshed in a specific culture, must, therefore, be on its guard, "in season and out of season" (2 Tim. 4:2). The Church proclaims the Gospel always with prayerful discernment, aware of its own frail, and sometimes blinded, condition. It must hold its prophets in high esteem. Often they will be counter-cultural: they see what others do not see. And they may indeed see the "-isms" in a specific culture before the official leaders of the Church do.

So long as evil exists in the world, the Church can never embrace a specific culture unconditionally; otherwise, it will find itself supporting and feeding that culture's "-isms," including racism and anti-Semitism. Clinging to the Word and the truths of revelation, the Church has to be enfleshed in a culture with a sometimes painful and discerning discretion. On occasion the Church will be happy to bless the goodness that God's grace has accomplished in God's created world, for "God looked at everything he had made and he found it very good" (Gen 1:31). When to bless and when to exorcise will be the Church's constant challenge in present society. But, in each culture, the Church needs to tread a careful line between one and the other. *The Pastoral Constitution on the Church in the Modern World* says it well: "Although he was made by God in a state of holiness, from the very dawn of history man abused his liberty, at the urging of personified Evil ... As a result, all of human life ... shows itself to be a struggle between good and evil."[40]

In the case of the Church's anti-Semitism, the Church, both in its theology and Liturgy, sinned against God's chosen people and against their culture. Pointedly, we observe that "Christian theologians who have assessed the role of anti-Judaism in the success of Nazi anti-Semitism note that *Christianity was undermined, even deformed, by its special animus toward Jews*."[41] The Church is on slippery ground as soon as it defines itself, or allows itself to be defined, in an "over-against" mode, i.e. against the Jews, the Masons, the Protestants, etc. This tendency of polar self-identification can become infected with a partial blindness that tends to

---

40. DVII, No. 13.

41. Peter Petit and John Townsend in *Seeing Judaism Anew*, 110. [Italics mine].

focus on perceived evil or heresy so much that it can no longer see the good. Yet, every heresy has some good or some truth in it, even though, due to our prejudice, we may not see it. This blinded focus often prevents non-judgmental listening, which is at the heart of true dialogue.

Yet, throughout its history, for its own self-preservation, the Church often had to define itself in an "over-against" mode. From the very beginning, the early Christian Church defined itself over against Rabbinic Judaism, even as the first Jewish Christians continued to worship, for a time, at the synagogues with their Jewish sisters and brothers. At the council of Nicea, in 325 CE, the official doctrine of the Church was defined over against anathematized Arianism, thereby preserving the dogma of Christ's divinity, a treasure of divine revelation, from being lost. In the Council of Trent, the true Catholic teaching was upheld against a powerful Protestant threat. Defending and preserving the fullness of God's revelation is no easy task, so there is no clear answer to this dilemma, except continuing dialogue, however imperfectly, with "the other side." The Church's contribution begins with the public confession of its own sinfulness, which it does during every Sunday Eucharist. True dialogue will soon change the Church's "over against" mode, building on the initial step forward that is repeated weekly in liturgical action.

What can we learn from the Church's encounter with the Latino/a and Jewish cultures? It has, at times, been a rough and tumultuous experience, for the Church, the Jewish people, and Latino/as. On the negative side, it is clear that the Spanish conquistadores imposed the Spanish culture, along with their Catholic religion, on the conquered natives of Latin America. Besides imposing their own religion, the Spanish imported their social caste system and imposed it upon the native population. Dictators, as history has shown us, like caste systems that assign to everyone their place in society. In these controlling systems, it is especially important that the poor 'know their place,' otherwise they may start a revolution. Caste systems, although they have a long history, are completely divorced from: "You shall love your neighbor as yourself" (Mt. 19:19); and, they are also far away from: "There is neither Jew nor Greek ... neither slave nor free ... neither male nor female" (Gal 3:28). Even more, they contradict the central Catholic symbol of the Eucharist: the breaking of bread and the sharing of the cup at a common table.

The conquering Spaniards also imposed the Spanish language and, in many cases, Spanish architecture. Although our survey is all too brief, in the case of the Jewish and Latino/a cultures, the Church's failures appear to outnumber its successes. Unless we name the failures, our Church runs the risk of repeating them. History is a great teacher, but only if we bow humbly and, sometimes, *penitentially* before its unvarnished truth. The Second Vatican Council worked hard to reduce the risk of repeating historical failures, by calling all Catholics to participate in the "The Proper Development of Culture." That will be the focus of our next chapter.

QUESTIONS FOR DISCUSSION

1. To what extent were you surprised by the history of anti-Semitism in the church? Do you feel there is any anti-Semitism in your parish today? In your community?

2. Do you feel the Church contributed to the Holocaust? Or, is this just anti-Catholic propaganda?

3. What steps can you and your parish take today to overcome anti-Semitism?

4. List some of the positive qualities that Latino/as have brought into our culture?

5. Do you feel there is any discrimination against Latino/as in your parish? Your community? What forms does it take? What can you do to overcome it?

6. Are the Latino/as well represented in your parish as lectors, Eucharistic ministers etc.?

7. How can you help undocumented Latino/as to become legal citizens?

4

Diagnosing our Cultures' Wounds

THE SECOND VATICAN COUNCIL, in the longest of its sixteen documents, devoted a whole chapter to "The Proper Development of Culture."[1] This is, indeed, a rich chapter in Part II of *The Pastoral Constitution on the Church in the Modern World*. And, we need to emphasize, this is a *Constitution*, not a simple *Decree* or *Declaration*. But so far, the average U.S. parish has not incorporated into its daily life the many changes this *Constitution* strongly recommends. No book on multiculturism would be complete without an in-depth discussion of the profound, and in some cases revolutionary, proposals contained in this section of the *Pastoral Constitution*.

A BRIEF HISTORY OF THE PASTORAL CONSTITUTION

The development of this *Constitution* was a long and complicated process. Prior to Vatican II, and certainly since the Council of Trent (1545–1563), the Church had been more concerned about its internal affairs than about its relation to the world, taking a defensive posture both in its doctrinal teaching and in its institutional discipline. The world 'out there' was considered to be either evil or neutral. In any case, there was little concern about the need 'to roll up our sleeves' and actually develop the world's cultures.

The writing of the *Pastoral Constitution* took considerable time and effort—altogether, seven drafts were produced. Among these seven were a Polish Text, prepared by Archbishop Karol Wojtyla and the Polish bishops, and the Malines Text, prepared by Cardinal Suenens and the Belgian bishops during their meetings in Malines, Belgium. A third text, called the Zurich Text, was written in French by theologians who met in Zurich. The final document still had to go through a dozen revisions before it was accepted.

---

1. DVII, No. 53.

Healing and Developing our Multiculturalism

Throughout the conciliar debates the bishops called for a more positive, less contemptuous, view of the world and its cultures. Many bishops repeated the theme that the Church's involvement in temporal affairs was part of its mission. The Church and poverty was a major theme of a forceful speech by Cardinal Lecaro: "First and foremost the Church must ever tend towards greater poverty," especially "evangelical poverty regarding ecclesiastical culture."[2]

The Cardinal's speech inspired other bishops to develop the theme of the Church in its relation to the world. Bishop Helder Camara, then Auxiliary Bishop of Rio de Janeiro, was especially upset at the Council's preoccupation with the Church's internal affairs:

> "He spoke often of the excessively internal character of the Council discussions: 'Are we to spend our whole time discussing internal Church problems while two-thirds of mankind is dying of hunger? What have we to say on the problems of underdevelopment? Will the Council express its concern about the great problems of mankind?'"[3]

These interventions were decisive in changing the attitudes of many bishops toward the world and its cultures.

Now the bishops were no longer in favor of building a strictly separatist Catholic culture, as in the 'old days,' or similar to the model of the Amish and Mennonite communities. Throughout the debates the emphasis was on Catholic cooperation in developing the world's cultures, mixed as always, with good and evil. Thus, the final text tells us: "... it is a duty most befitting our times that men, especially Christians, should work strenuously on behalf of certain decisions which must be made in the economic and political fields, both nationally and internationally."[4] There is no hint of flight from the "evil" world.

Within the bishops' discussions, we may note some tensions between the deductive and inductive methods, between a theological and a sociological approach. Many bishops, because of their "top-down" theological training, were just not used to the inductive method; in fact, they were uncomfortable with reflections on the nitty-gritty, earthy conditions of

---

2. Tanner, *The Church and the World*, 24.

3. Vorgrimler, ed., *Commentary on the Documents of Vatican II*, 11. [Hereafter cited as CDVII].

4. DVII, No. 60.

poverty or "the findings of the secular sciences, especially of psychology and sociology." These bishops wanted a more abstract, theological tone. They were in favor of proclaiming general principles without going into the failures of the present human conditions in the various cultures, especially the poverty of the developing countries.

Other bishops, in contrast, thought the text was too positive about the condition of the modern world; for them, there was not enough emphasis on sin in the world. Not a few felt the text was too much a reflection of the wealthy West. For many bishops the whole text was too European. On the more positive side, there was a growing emphasis on reading "the signs of the times," a favorite theme of Pope John XXIII. Of course, this meant that the inductive method and sociology got more attention. It also meant more emphasis on the rights of all human beings, regardless of their status in society. Many bishops wanted the text to emphasize that human dignity is God-given by nature. The final text says: "A man is more precious for what he is than for what he has."[5] Respect and reverence for human dignity forms the basis for recommending a "sincere and prudent" dialogue with atheists.[6]

During the discussions on marriage and the family Cardinal Dearden of Detroit announced that Pope Paul VI had decided to reserve the birth control issue to himself. That issue, therefore, was never explicitly discussed in the Council. So, to the consternation of many bishops, the Council omitted addressing one of the burning issues of the day. Pope Paul VI, after much agonizing, issued his famous "Birth Control" encyclical, *Humanae Vitae*, in August, 1968; resistance to, and sometimes, rejection of, that encyclical is well known. There was, as well, an additional element of contention within this part of the Council, as some speakers wanted the distinguished Barbara Ward to address the Council when it was discussing marriage and family. But Archbishop Felici, the secretary general of the Council, "indicated that it would be 'premature' for a woman to address the Council."[7]

Discussion on the *Pastoral Constitution* was quite lively to the very end. On the last day of the Council, however, when the final votes were counted, there were 2,309 in favor and only 75 against. Considering the

---

5. DVII, No. 35.
6. Ibid., No. 21.
7. Tanner, *The Church and the World*, 26.

newness and variety of topics covered, this *Pastoral Constitution* is, no doubt, one of the greatest achievements of the Second Vatican Council.

SOME PRINCIPLES FOR THE DEVELOPMENT OF CULTURES

The time has come to get practical and find out exactly what we are expected to do when we 'roll up our sleeves' and start developing our culture. As the *Constitution* urges, "culture is an immediately evident and essential feature of human life, a universal fact: 'Man is by nature a cultural entity. Wherever there is man, there is culture.'"[8] Here, we need to recall the *Constitution's* general definition: "... 'culture' indicates all those factors by which man refines and unfolds his manifold spiritual and bodily qualities."[9] Thus, before we can refine or develop a culture, we have to find out first what in human life needs to be repaired, what needs to be healed. As this all too brief diagnosis will reveal, some parts of our human culture are broken and need to be repaired. There are many structural problems, deep wounds in our culture, which need to be healed. Only then can we begin the refining and developing process. When we break a bone in our bodies, it first needs to be repaired or re-set, before the healing can begin. After that, the previously broken bone is ready for development. This chapter will attempt a brief diagnosis of our culture's wounds. The next chapter will then offer suggestions for healing and developing our culture. But, as we know, successful healing and developing depends on an accurate diagnosis.

So what principles do we follow? Is there a blueprint available for diagnosing the wounds of a culture? Or, do we have to develop our own? Does our long Christian tradition point the way? If we are going to cooperate in repairing, healing, and developing our existing culture, how do we discern what needs to be done? What are the active dynamics shaping our present culture? How do we grab them, to bend or influence them one way or the other? Or, are they just too powerful, too overwhelming? Are we ready and willing to take on a modern Goliath? Or, on the other hand, is saving grace, "our new creation," our new David, the more powerful dynamic on this spinning earth? Or, finally, are we so habitually stuck in passivity that we do not know how, or do not have the will, to give the power of divine grace a try? For some answers to these questions, we

8. CDVII, 255.
9. DVII, No. 53.

will rely mostly on Chapter II of Part II of the *Pastoral Constitution on the Church in the Modern World*, which, as noted above, is entitled: "The Proper Development of Culture."

The first principle proclaimed in this chapter states that we are called "to *community*."[10] After the enfleshment of the God-man in Jesus, the "human" is fundamentally reoriented and given a new capacity. Redeemed by Jesus Christ and called to holiness, every human is capable of living a life in Christ and is destined to rise with Him. Humans are also social animals and therefore live a social life in family and community. Developing a culture, therefore, necessarily includes our human social community.

This principle reminds us of the Thomistic axiom that grace perfects nature. We are also heirs to that profound biblical principle of holy creation: "God saw everything that he had made, and indeed, it was very good" (Gen 1:31). Thus, there is no room for the dualism of Zoroastrianism, Gnosticism, Manichaeanism, or Albigensianism. The human, material world, though wounded, is still "good," and there is room and need for building better cultures. In fact, since the Incarnation, the human is an apt vehicle or instrument for the divine. Of course, sin, as St. Paul reminds us, entered into God's holy creation, and so existing culture, even after the Incarnation, is always a mixture of good and evil, and will be until the Kingdom of God arrives. And that will be our challenge as we build a better family and community culture; it will require continuous prayerful discernment. Flight from a grey, ambiguous world into dualism is an easy and constant temptation. Christian engagement with the world's messy structures needs to lean heavily on faith in the power of grace and the Holy Spirit to overcome evil. That is the second principle for the proper development of our mixed culture.

DIAGNOSING SOME OF OUR CULTURES' WOUNDS

First, we need to reflect prayerfully on what is wrong with our culture as it is. If we, as Christians, were running the U.S. and its culture, what would we fix first? In view of revelation through Christ, what are the wounds that infect our culture? Since we are immersed in our culture, these wounds or diseases are also part of us. History and our own conscience will testify that we, as Christians, are not immune to the pathologies of our temporal world. Even the brilliant St. Augustine, who gave us a blueprint in the *City*

---

10. Ibid. [Italics mine].

of God (430), tolerated slavery as the result of our sinful human condition, though it was not approved by God. The criteria we use to diagnose our culture's sickness will always be the Gospel and our living Christian tradition in the present teaching of the Church. It is only by applying these criteria that we can discern what are the ills in our society and cultures.

POSTMODERNITY

Many theologians agree that our culture has transitioned into the age of postmodernity. This term is a broad umbrella that includes both positive and negative elements. By way of introduction to this slippery term, we will reflect on the descriptive definition of Roger Haight, S.J. His definition applies primarily, although not exclusively, to the members of the church insofar as they have absorbed both the weeds and the wheat in the 'culture' of postmodernity. Haight's criteria flow from Christology, broadly considered. He is wrestling with the question: How do we teach Christology to a postmodern Christian? In this, Haight relies on a variety of authors who treat postmodernity in depth in its variety of meanings and applications.[11] We will be concerned primarily about how postmodernity affects our Christian call to develop today's culture, accepting the reality that we ourselves are immersed in postmodernity.

First, as noted earlier in the introduction, Roger Haight tells us, "postmodernity involves a radical historical consciousness. Gone is the confidence in progress, goals toward which history is heading [the hallmark of Enlightenment thought] ... The twentieth century has added ... a new sense of evil and collective human sin: it has been a century of war and human destructiveness."[12] Haight continues: "Second, postmodernity involves a critical social consciousness ... society is driven by little more than the interests of power, or class, or gender, or greed. This side of postmodernity threatens a loss of the human subject, of the person who is reduced to a function of impersonal forces."[13] Therefore, developing a more human culture will require a constant awareness of the God-given dignity of the human person. In those cases where the human person becomes just one more cog in the

---

11. See especially Lakeland, *Postmodernity: Christian Identity in a Fragmented Age*; and, Terrence W. Tilley, *Postmodern Theologies: The Challenge of Religious Diversity*.

12. Haight, *Jesus Symbol of God*, 331.

13. Ibid., 332.

wheel of the industrial machine, proper development of our culture will require resistance to reducing the human person to a commodity.

Haight demonstrates, thirdly, that "postmodernity involves a pluralist consciousness ... One can no longer claim western culture as the center, the higher point of view, or Christianity as the superior religion ... The world is pluralistic and polycentric in its horizons of interpretation."[14] So, we should not be surprised that our culture no longer believes in 'absolute' or 'universal' values. This means that our world culture spins and turns on passing personal opinions. These opinions come to us through the media in the forms they choose, mostly through TV's glossy images.

A further change brought by postmodernity is one which "involves a cosmic consciousness ... Astronomy and the physical sciences have transformed the picture of the cosmos and of the place of our galaxy and planet in it ... One cannot operate with a language that tacitly presumes an Aristotelian universe."[15] The television brings us daily news of global warming and its effects on our weather systems; it also brings us the pain and tears of all the people whose lives are uprooted by hurricanes and earthquakes, whether in New Orleans or Indonesia. We are now more conscious of the need to take care of our global environment. The stakes are high in this situation: our civilization will live or die, depending on our human care of God's holy creation. All of this is the product of a growing cosmic or global consciousness.

Other pathologies, in addition to the ones we will explore below, could be added to the list of cultural ills that have become immediately apparent in the conditions opened by postmodernity. Some of the following "-isms" may overlap a little, and they may not give us the complete picture. Thus, there is no intention to explore these "-isms" in any depth. In most cases, such an analysis would require several books alone. But even a brief review of some of our culture's ills may help the reader's own discernment process.

ABORTION

Abortion has rightly been called "an unspeakable crime," both by the Second Vatican Council and by the American bishops. Yet, in 2006, there were 126,000 abortions performed per day, totaling 46 million per year.

14. Ibid., 333.
15. Ibid., 334.

This crime is becoming so common that, unfortunately, our culture no longer considers it a crime. Our conscience as a community has lost its reverence for life as a gift from God. In the process, our culture has lost its respect for life as such, whatever its form or stage of development. Perhaps the most powerful, and, at the same time, the most succinct statement on abortion comes from the American bishops' Pastoral Letter of 1975:

> Respect for human life has been gradually declining in our society during the past decade. To some degree this reflects a secularizing trend and a rejection of moral imperatives based on belief in God and His plan for creation. It also reflects a tendency for individuals to give primary attention to what is personally rewarding and satisfying to them, to the exclusion of responsible concern for the well-being of other persons and society. These trends, along with others have resulted in laws and judicial decisions which deny or ignore basic human rights and moral responsibilities for the protection and promotion of the common good.[16]

Abortion is a sword in our culture's womb. Many books could be written on the implications for our culture resulting from this deep wound in our society and our nation. But so far, we have not developed an effective system for educating either adults, or the young in our schools on the holiness and moral implications of human sexuality. And, we might add, so far, the teaching of the church on sexuality at the parish level continues to be more negative than positive. Abortion represents a selfish and self-destructive disease. We rightly appropriate considerable funds and energy for a cure for AIDS and cancer, but, so far, our government has not allocated any public funds for a solution to the problem of abortion. Moral self-discipline, which is plainly missing today, is one of the great pillars of a strong and healthy culture.

WOMEN IN U.S. CULTURE

The governing pattern of our social structure has been called misogyny—hatred or distrust of women. Hatred may seem like a strong word, but misogyny, as hatred, is probably the most honest description of this deep wound, which infects most of the cultures on this earth. Misogyny has a long history, going back at least to Aristotle. Aristotle (384–322 BCE) taught

---

16. "*Pastoral Plan for Pro-Life Activities*," in *Pastoral Letters of the United States Catholic Bishops*, vol. 4, ed. Hugh Nolan, 81.

that the concept of purpose is fundamental to all living things, and that men and women have different purposes. According to Aristotle, "the male is by nature superior and the female inferior; and the one rules, and the other is ruled; the principle of necessity extends to all mankind ... The female is, as it were, a mutilated male."[17] In the Aristotelian paradigm, "the male is the active principle, the mover, the female the passive, the moved."[18]

Aristotle was such a powerful influence that many cultures, both in the East and in the West, uncritically accepted his flawed teaching. Thus, even the brilliant St. Thomas Aquinas accepted Aristotle's teaching that women were *by nature* inferior. Aquinas writes in his *Summa Theologica:*

> As regards the individual, woman is defective and misbegotten, for the active force in the male seed tends to the reproduction of a perfect likeness in the masculine sex while the production of woman comes from a defect in the active force or from some material disposition or even from some external influence; such as that of the south wind which is moist, as the Philosopher observes.[19]

Aristotle and St. Thomas Aquinas, no doubt, deserve a high grade in philosophy, but they both fail biology, at least as we are now aware. Nevertheless, through the vast influence of Aquinas, Aristotle's misogyny gained a philosophical and theological foothold that nourished and spread this oldest prejudice through most of the world's cultures. And, we have to admit, that Christianity played an important role in spreading that prejudice. Christianity became the vehicle for transporting Aquinas' Aristotelian-derived misogyny across the Catholic world. The persistence of this viewpoint is rooted in its global vision, in providing an explanatory way of reading the world and its structures, teaching that women's inferior status is part of the natural order. And, of course, this teaching gave the firmest ground for why things are they way that they are: God was the Creator of that unchangeable natural order. While this teaching was not a central or necessary part of Christian revelation, it became imbedded in the Christian culture through the teaching of a static and perennial Catholic philosophy.

While Greek patriarchy accounts for much of the initial ground of the social vision of misogyny, the Roman Empire also provided a fertile

---

17. Holland. *Misogyny.* 33.
18. Ibid.
19. Aquinas, *Summa Theologica*, Ia.Q92.a1.rep.1.

environment for its growth. In the Roman Empire, however, misogyny took a less philosophical and more legalistic turn. Roman women protested their inferior status, so the Roman Empire reacted by passing more laws regarding the behavior of women.

> In early Rome, circa the seventh century BC, they (women) were subject to some of the most oppressive marriage laws imaginable. As a wife, a woman was placed under the absolute rule of her husband, who had the power of life or death over her. Sitting in judgment with his wife's relatives, a husband was 'given the power to pass sentence in cases of adultery and . . . if any wife was found drinking wine, Romulus allowed the death penalty for both crimes.'"[20]

These laws were rooted in the Roman form of patriarchy and its distinction between *potestas* (power) and *auctoritas* (authority). In the Roman culture there was a great distinction between the two concepts. The husband had *potestas* or power; the wife had only *auctoritas* or authority. Thus, power meant strength, might or control over something. Power was personal: if the husband went off to war, power went with him. The male had the power of life or death over his wife and children. Authority, on the other hand, meant approval or assent. Thus, the wife, like the Roman Senate, had only the authority to assent or to approve. She had the authority to approve or disapprove her husband's actions, but the husband had the power to ignore, and often did, his wife's approval or non-approval. The husband could drown a female baby in the river, even while his wife was screaming her disapproval. The wife's authority was consultative only. Strangely, the husband, sometimes by law, had to consult his wife, but having consulted, he could do as he pleased. In practice consultation was no limit to his power.

In the early Roman Empire female infanticide was quite common. Romulus "decreed that only 'every male child and the first-born female' be reared– an invitation to expose (kill) other daughters born afterwards."[21] The father could kill legally all female babies except the first one. Husbands had the power, and wives did not. Women were just a notch above slaves, both in the Greek and Roman Empires. The notion of the equality of the sexes was not considered in cultures where slavery and inequality were natural, legal, and institutionalized. But, the Greek and Roman cultures

---

20. Holland, *Misogyny*, 39.
21. Ibid. 38.

were not the only cultures guilty of misogyny. They were simply part of a world in which misogyny was the accepted norm.

While it is impossible to do a survey of women's role in all the cultures, we would be remiss if we overlooked China. Here, the inferior status of women had a religious basis in the teaching of Confucius. In this, all relationships were modeled on the paradigm of subject to ruler, or son to father. Relationships were construed as between a superior and a subordinate.[22] The social structure was fundamentally based on hierarchy. As late as the 1930s, the subjection of women was symbolized by the custom of foot binding. This custom involved tightly wrapping women's outside three toes and bending them back towards the ball of the foot. The goal was to achieve a small "Lotus Foot." A woman with small feet was considered beautiful. Of course, this was one form of crippling women, distorting their step. The cruel custom of foot binding was not banned until 1949.[23]

There were other customs, in addition, which maintained the low status of Chinese women. We read in Confucius' Book of Rites a prohibition against physical contact between the sexes: "A man and woman shall not give anything directly one to the other from hand to hand. If a man gives something to a woman, she receives it on a bamboo tray."[24] China, as well, allowed polygamy through most of its history. It was not uncommon for men to have three or even a dozen wives and concubines. In fact, polygamy was the norm until 1912 when it was finally outlawed. Women in Chinese culture were deliberately kept illiterate, and were barred from involvement in the political structure. Holland reports that "women were not allowed to take part in government affairs"[25] However, since the 1990's, a sexual revolution, similar to those in Western countries, has been sweeping through China, and centuries of repression of women seem to be coming to an end.

With such a long history of misogyny in the world's cultures, we should not be surprised that our own history, in U.S. culture, demonstrates a similar tale. The process of healing in regard to this issue, within the U.S., has been a slow, but steady affair. After a long state-by-state struggle

22. Fairbank and Goodman, *China*, 19.
23. Holland, *Misogyny*, 175.
24. Ibid., 173.
25. Ibid., 174.

for women's suffrage, a constitutional amendment was passed on June 5, 1919, giving women the right to vote. Fortunately, many churches have been active on the front of women's issues. The Episcopal Church, amid expected controversy, has ordained women as bishops. In the Catholic Church, the Women's Ordination Conference held its first meeting in 1975, and has been meeting annually ever since. WomanChurch was founded in 1983; the specific goal of this group is a church free from patriarchy and sexism.

Though there have been considerable gains, the gender issue in the Catholic Church has been hardly free from tumult. For nine years, beginning in 1988, the American Catholic Bishops tried, with wide consultation of women, to publish a Pastoral Letter on the role of women in the church. The controversy that followed is impossible to compress in these few pages. Suffice it to say, that the proposed letter was never published. But, we can say, tentatively, that today women are making considerable progress in obtaining and holding leadership positions in the church, both at the diocesan and parish levels. The Official Catholic Directory of 2006 reports the following statistics regarding women's ministries in the Catholic Church:

> 25% of all diocesan chancellors
> 80% of all lay ecclesial ministers
> 40% of all parish Liturgy planners
> 65% of all parish music ministers
> 88% of all parish religious educators
> 54% of all parish RCIA directors
> 63% of all participants in lay ecclesial formation.[26]

This list provides compelling evidence that the Catholic communities across the nation are implementing St. Paul's teaching that competence and leadership qualities are *not dependent on gender or ordination* (1 Cor 12:4–11). The church has had leadership from the beginning, but it did not have a Sacrament of ordination in our modern sense until Peter Lombard in the twelfth century.[27]

As of this writing, the United Nations is pushing hard to persuade all nations to sign a Convention that would eliminate all forms of discrimination against women. So far, 185 countries, including China, have pledged

---

26. The CARA Report, V. 12, No. 2.
27. Joseph Martos, *Doors to the Sacred*, 495.

to adopt this policy of women's equality in their cultures. This means that women will have the same rights as men, including the right to equal pay. The Convention includes a requirement that all countries report to the U.N., every four years, on the status of women in their countries. So there is some progress being made on healing this cultural wound in the modern world.

In view of the creation story in Genesis and the Pauline letters, Christians need to face the moral implications of misogyny and the imposition of inferior, unequal status upon women, both in churches and in cultures. Genesis 1:27 tells us that "God created the human in His image; in the divine image He created the human; male and female He created them." Modern scripture scholars understand "Adam," in this Genesis account, not as a single, historical individual, but as a symbolic figure of the human being. Thus, "Adam" has to represent both human genders, and, in this, one gender cannot be less equal than another. There is no hint in the Genesis account that the creation of two genders introduces any distinction of status: both genders make up "the human."

St. Paul, in Col 1–15, tells us that the risen Christ is the "image (Greek=icon) of the invisible God." But, then he goes on to say that Christ "is the first-born of all creation; for in him all things were created in heaven and on earth, visible and invisible ... for in Him all the fullness of God was pleased to dwell." In the risen Christ we have an image, an icon, of everything ever created in "heaven and on earth." It is clear that, for Paul, the risen Christ is the image or icon of the whole created human race (obviously including both genders). In 1 Cor 15:45, Paul writes: "Just as we have borne the image (icon) of the man of dust, we shall also bear the image (icon) of the man of heaven." To say that one half of this human race is of a lesser status than the other is to do serious violence to the heavenly icon that is the risen Christ. As Paul tells us, "for God was in Christ reconciling the world to Himself" (2 Cor 5:19). This reconciled world includes all creatures of whatever gender. Thus, discrimination on the basis of gender is both a denial of the Genesis account and a denial of the fullness of the Resurrection of Christ. Even more, it is a denial of the eschatological purpose of humanity—deification. Transformed through the Resurrection, the risen Christ is the glorification of the divinized human, male and female.

Overcoming entrenched misogyny and achieving gender equality at all levels of the U.S. culture remains a continuing challenge. The next chapter will offer a few suggestions for healing this wound.

INDIVIDUALISM

No one can doubt that individualism dominates the U.S. culture of today. Almost everyone has their own car, TV, computer and cell phone. Car-pooling is rare, reflecting the fact that everyone wants their independence; and, as a result, our "expressways" are clogged every morning by cars– empty except for the driver. The end products of this way of life are pollution and road rage. Even within our homes, the influence of individualism is quite visible: most homes have at least two or more televisions sets, some even have four or five, all so that everyone can watch their own programs—alone. Children are glued to their favorite games or sites on the Internet, even during "family" meals. With the multiplication of cell phones, children can be isolated in their bedrooms, talking only to their friends. Affluence means we don't have to borrow anyone's tools or toys: we have our own. *The inalienable right to privacy is our culture's new gospel*, and, because of this, we forget that by nature we are social animals. Meanwhile, the rights of the common good, including the poor, are lost to the privatized space.

Individualism has also infected our religious communities, which are publicly committed to the common good and to building community:

> As a 'religious term' individualism can be defined 'as a tendency to reduce Christianity to the vertical relation between God and the individual person,' leading to 'a one sided emphasis upon individual freedom, competence, and self-reliance ... the Enlightenment stressed the competence of the individual's reason and conscience ... making intuition authoritative in morals and religion ...The consequences are subjectivism ... the proliferation of sectarian divisions ... and loss of awareness that the church of Jesus Christ exists for service and that this ministry is shared by all members.'[28]

Vatican II's call to build a more human community will have to deal with both secular and religious individualism. It may, at times, seem like an

---

28. T. C. O'Brien, ed., *The Encyclopedic Dictionary of the Western Churches*, 393.

insurmountable obstacle. But, as always, our risen Christ will help us overcome this poison in our culture and community.

RELATIVISM

Pope Benedict XVI, in his homily before the conclave that elected him, (April 20, 2005) gave a brief introduction to this complicated philosophical principle: "Relativism is letting oneself be swept along by every wind of teaching. It looks like the only attitude (acceptable) to today's standards. We are moving toward a dictatorship of relativism, which does not recognize anything as certain and which has as its highest goal one's own ego and one's own desires."

Perhaps, for Christians, the most serious impact of relativism comes in the field of ethics, since it "denies the existence of universally obligatory norms of morality."[29] Thus the individual or society and civilization become the 'measure of all things.' In other words, the individual and culture determine what is right and wrong. There is no need for revelation, for the Ten Commandments, or even a 'higher spiritual authority.' Everything is relative to *me*; what works for *me* has become the supreme norm. Along with individualism, relativism is a serious obstacle to forming community, both civil and religious. The glue of common bonds is missing. Once again, an awareness of the priority of the common good, both in the government and in civil society, vanishes altogether.

THE IDOLATRIES OF CONSUMERISM

I have always been intrigued by the fact that the first of the Ten Commandments is not about sex, but about idolatry. It seems that the God of Mt. Sinai figured that idolatry was going to be a more serious problem than sex. So, the first commandment given is "you shall not have other gods besides me... you shall not carve idols for yourselves...you shall not bow down and worship them" (Exod 20:2–4).

The argument may seem a little subtle at times, but John Kavanaugh is clear enough; he writes that in our obsession to consume things, our "carved images," we have become the things we consume, such that "our being is in having and doing. Our happiness is said to be in possessing more."[30] We have allowed ourselves to be reduced to commodities, and

---

29. Karl Rahner, ed., *Sacramentum Mundi*, s.v. "Relativism," 5: 242.
30. Kavanaugh, *Following Christ in a Consumer Society*, 64–72.

being a commodity becomes a form of life. Our 'carved idols' have become our life because we let them; and, in so doing, they in turn consume us. Kavanaugh, quite correctly, calls this the Commodity Form of Life, as opposed to the Personal Form of Life. In the commoditized lifestyle, "those who make idols and put their trust in them become like them . . . Such is the result of idolatry."[31]

Large companies and marketers are quite aware they can use us as commodities. The curvy young lady selling that car on TV is being used by the marketer as a commodity. For a little money, a commodity, she lets herself be used. The heroes on the athletic field are the "carved idols" being used to sell athletic shoes and T-shirts. The Hollywood "heroes" are the marketers' commodities for selling swimsuits. We worship violence on film and TV, and then we reenact that violence on our city streets, and on the battlefields of our own making. This is all part of the Commodity Form of Life. We become commodities. We become the clay idol molded by the mighty god of consumerism, which becomes the idol we worship.

The ritual of the Christmas stampede to Wal-mart is a good visual definition of consumerism, and a demonstration of our compulsive pursuit of commodities. Our former rural culture, with much sweat and blood, was immersed in producing; now our culture is obsessed with consuming, often inflicting sweat and blood in the mad rushes and throngs of sales departments. Large companies pay large sums of money to persuade people they have many needs. Besides, that the people want to keep up with their neighbors. So our shopping carts are overflowing with Wal-mart's response to artificially created wants and needs. One bumper sticker tells one half the story: "Today is the last day for shopping until tomorrow;" another reveals the more serious side: "I shop, therefore I am."[32] Shopping has become one of the vital signs of self-awareness, self-consciousness, and self- identity.

Shopping obsession, a hallmark of a consumer driven society, is in reality a numbing agent, much like Novocain, filling an interior or spiritual void with a shopping cart full of material things. "Bereft of any interior life and starved for relationship," writes John Kavanaugh, "it is only logical that we feel driven to fill the emptiness that is within us and the absence

---

31. Ibid., 68.
32. Quoted in John F. Kavanaugh. *Following Christ in a Consumer Society*, 12.

that is between us ... Buying and consuming have become the vehicles for experiencing the sacred."³³

These shoppers have not yet internalized the meaning of a basic truth of our Christian Faith: "For where your inmost thirst would take you, the fountains of earth have ceased to flow; where your last nostalgia fades blue, all the clocks of time are stopped."³⁴

Twenty-five years ago, our American Bishops alerted us to the deep wound of consumerism plaguing the U.S. culture:

> Our obsessive consumerism ... leads us to use up a far greater share of the earth's resources than any other country in history, makes poorer nations look upon us as the wastrels of this world. It is not merely envy but rightful indignation about our spending habits that accounts for the little friendship we generally receive from the poor nations. Such habits are particularly objectionable in the followers of Him who had no stone on which to rest His head.³⁵

Though written almost three decades ago, the bishops' words are as valid today as they were then. But, many economists say consuming is what keeps our American economy humming. Materialistic economic theories, not moral or spiritual values, are what shape U.S. culture.

Andrew Bacevich describes the post-war shift in our U.S. culture toward an Empire of Consumption: "In *Among Empires*, author Charles Maier ... has chronicled the shift from what he calls America's postwar Empire of Production—when we made the steel, the cars, and the TVs—to today's Empire of Consumption—when goods pour in from Japan and China."³⁶ This is a significant shift within our culture. So far, our culture does not realize the implications of living in an Empire in which the higher Christian values, like an interior life and helping the poor, are sacrificed on the altar of consumption.

"Marketers," according to *The U.S. New and World Report* (Nov. 13, 2006), "are throwing money at all kinds of new advertising models in an effort to get noticed by over-pitched consumers. Companies spent 53.4 million on alternative advertising such as pitches in video games or mobile phones during the first half of this year." Submissive before the

---

33. Ibid., 13.
34. Gertrude von Le Fort. *Hymns to the Church*, 18.
35. *"Pastoral Letter on Marxist Communism,"* in *Pastoral Letters*, IV: 399.
36. Bacevich, "Twilight of the Republic," Commonweal 133/21 (December 2006): 11.

marketers' onslaught, we devour new gadgets, like the latest iPod, as if life could not go on without it. While the poor are starving, we spend $34 billion a year on our pets. Marketers are now focusing on "pet attire;" no doubt, America's pets will soon be wearing mink coats and monogrammed sweaters.[37]

The marketers' drumbeat has its effect on all of us—an unavoidable reality of our market driven society. Growth of obsessive, compulsive hoarding is the cumulative, net result of life in society structured around commodities and markets. "According to Mental Health America," as of 2007," more than 2 million Americans are hoarders ... 1 in 11 households rent storage space—1 million more households than two years ago."[38] Likely, there is some research indicating a connection between hoarding and shoplifting.

The most important step in diagnosing consumerism as a wound in our culture is to reflect long and hard on "The Commodity Form of Life." John Kavanaugh does a masterful job in explaining the "Commodity Form" of life by opposing it to "The Personal Form" of life.[39] Thus, in the Commodity Form, values are grounded in Thinghood; in the Personal Form, values are grounded in personhood. To survive this onslaught with our own Christian values intact, we simply have to develop a stout, prophetic resistance to this daily bombardment by the media. At the same time, we have to bend our energies to recover the priority of the Christian values that will heal and sustain a healthy culture.

LACK OF AWARENESS OF THE COMMON GOOD

In light of the fierce hold of individualism on our society, as described above, we should not be surprised that the common good suffers the most in our culture. No politicians have the common good as the focus of their platform for election. We do not see it discussed on TV or in the daily paper. There are no public protests for the common good. Not even bumper stickers! The phrase is missing in our public discourse. This is a deep wound both in our democracy and in our culture. Discussions on social

---

37. Kavanaugh, *Following Christ in a Consumer Society*, 20.

38. Gettelman, "No Sex Please, We're Organizing," *Mother Jones* 32 (July–August, 2007), 20–21.

39. Kavanaugh, 24–26.

justice will get nowhere until the public becomes conscious, in a moral sense, of the role the common good plays in a healthy society.

Human beings are social animals. To achieve a healthy life we need to live in active relationships within a society. We contribute to society, and society, in turn, contributes to our welfare. And that is where the common good is most at play. The common good has been defined as:

> ... the complex of spiritual, temporal, and material conditions needed in society if each person is to have the opportunity to develop his or her human potential ... The public order is that part of the common good that properly belongs to the state. It is constituted by the goods of public peace, public morality, and the enforcement of basic standards of justice ...[40]

This definition deliberately makes an important distinction between the state and society. Thus, the role of the state is limited to the public order. Of course, the state and society need to cooperate in caring for the common good. "Society" here includes "churches, families, private educational and civic associations, business corporations, labor unions."[41]

The church, for many years, has been a lonely voice speaking and writing on behalf of the common good. In May 1931, Pope Pius XI published his powerful encyclical, *Quadragesimo Anno*, 40 years after Pope Leo XIII's wonderful *Rerum Novarum*. Both encyclicals deal primarily with labor problems and social justice issues. "To lower or raise wages unduly," writes Pope Pius XI, "with a view to private profit, and with *no consideration for the common good,* is contrary to social justice which demands that by union of effort and good will such a scale of wages be set up, if possible, as to offer the greatest number of opportunities of employment and of securing for themselves suitable means of livelihood."[42] Employers, labor unions and the state need to work together for the common good of society. The thirty-seven million living below poverty level are still waiting for justice and are still in need of help.

Unfortunately, these two major papal encyclicals are virtually unknown or unread in today's world. But, doing nothing is not an answer or solution to the problem. As a first step, we can all join The Catholic

---

40. Quoted in *American Catholics and Civic Engagement*, ed. Margaret O'Brien Steinfels, 53.

41. John Coleman, "The Common Good and Catholic Social Thought," in *American Catholics and Civic Engagement*, 16.

42. *The Five Great Encyclicals*, ed. Gerald Treacy, 146. [Italics mine].

Alliance for the Common Good (www.thecatholicalliance.org.) This organization holds out "four principles for public life: 1) We are all in this together; 2) Preferential protection to the most vulnerable in society; 3) Good governance; and, 4) Principles before profit and power."[43] The Alliance is dedicated to promoting awareness of the Catholic Tradition and its core values of justice, human dignity and the common good to Catholics, the media and Americans of all faiths. By joining together with this cause, we may, as their website indicates, heighten awareness concerning the issues of social justice, faith, and public life.

EMPIRICISM AS AN ABSOLUTE

The roots of Empiricism can be traced all the way back to Aristotle, insofar as he presupposed an ability to perceive the world around us by means of the senses. The famous slogan, "there is nothing in the intellect that was not previously in the senses," has been attributed to Aristotle himself. But that empiricist phrase became part of the scholastic system with the help of St. Thomas Aquinas. Aquinas contributed the classical Latin form of empirical philosophy: "*Nihil in intellectu quod non prius fuerit in sensu.*"[44] So, in Catholic philosophy, a form of empiricism has been given a place, but its place is clearly defined. Catholic philosophy rejects Descartes' teaching, when "he insists that our senses, even when they are in perfect working order, are still inherently unreliable informants about the true nature of reality."[45] Yes, the senses can be wrong, but they are not "inherently unreliable."

In distinction from Catholic philosophy, empiricism was taught as an independent philosophical system, primarily by the English and Scottish philosophers John Locke (1632–1704) and David Hume (1711–76). For them, empiricism meant, in general, that experience alone is the true foundation of knowledge and science. Basically, empiricism is about the problem of epistemology, or the nature and ground of knowledge. Thus, if men, logically including male obstetricians, have never themselves given birth to a baby, they know nothing about it. We just have to experience it ourselves to have real knowledge about anything. In the extreme form, we have to feel,

---

43. Alexia Kelley, *"Challenge of the Common Good,"* Network Connection, 34, (Nov./Dec. 2006), 6–7.

44. Cottingham, *Rationalism*, 27–28.

45. Ibid., 39.

touch, hear, taste or see it, before we know anything about anything. Without the verifiable testimony of the senses, knowledge is not knowledge.

This theory spread to the U.S. through the influence of the Scottish common sense philosophical movement of the eighteenth and nineteenth centuries. The long-term effect of empiricism, tinged with a pinch of skepticism, is the elimination of faith in the unseen world. Some modern authors, who do not believe in faith or religion, routinely demand: "Where's the evidence?"[46] "Evidence (whether sensory or logical)," Sam Harris argues, in his recent volume, "is the *only thing* that suggests that a given belief is really about the world..."[47] Reflecting the skeptical shape of contemporary American culture, Harris' book has become a massive *New York Times* bestseller. The theory that what is real is only that which is known with the senses and is an object of experience is deeply ingrained in our present day society. Thus, there is no room for an unseen, infinite, and transcendent God; likewise, there is no room for faith or invisible grace. And faith, in this theory, excludes reason—faith is reason's exact opposite. In the closing of the American mind to faith and the unseen, there is no allowance for both/and, only either/or. This black or white approach makes good fodder for today's dualistic fundamentalism.

SECULARISM

This "-ism" has a confusing variety of applications, but, in general, it may be defined as a "form of humanism that limits the true value to those temporal qualities that contribute to man's natural perfection, both individual and social, to the actual exclusion of the supernatural."[48] Secularism is a philosophy of life "and, in the broad sense of the word, a religion, independent of revealed religion." The U.S. Bishops, in 1947, wrote that secularism "may be described as a view of life that limits itself not to the material in exclusion of the spiritual, but to the human here and now to the exclusion of man's relation to God here and hereafter."[49]

However, the bishops' definition of secularism, published well before Vatican II's *Pastoral Constitution in the Modern World*, needs to be inter-

---

46. See Harris, *The End of Faith*.
47. Ibid., 71–72.
48. *The Catholic Encyclopedia*, ed. Catholic University of America, 5: 13, 37.
49. *Pastoral Letters of the United States Catholic Bishops*, "Statement on Secularism," II: 74.

preted in the light of this document. The human being, here and now, according to the *Pastoral Constitution*, is holy, created by an all holy God and redeemed by Christ. Since Vatican II, theologians have proposed a more positive, less condemnatory, view of the world and the whole area of the so-called secular. "What is at stake," explains the *Encyclopedia of Theology* "is the true secularity of the world, which consists of the truth that there is nothing in the world which is too 'holy' to be accessible to a worldly approach and must be reserved for religion."[50] The *Encyclopedia* continues: "The Christian enjoys the freedom of the children of God through Christ and is lord of the world, where everything is holy and unholy at the same time according to how truly it is in Christ…"[51] And again, "there is nothing in the structure of the world which is taboo, which is to be removed from man's use."[52] Secularism is evil only when it, positively and explicitly, excludes the presence of God from 'the human.' Since humanity was created holy by an all-holy God, it remains basically holy in spite of human sin. So, secularism is a confusing mixture of holy creation and unholy human sin. The Christian challenge is to distinguish one from the other, to develop the one and eliminate the other, which will require considerable prayerful discernment. It is easy to fall into the trap of seeing evil more clearly than the good. The evening news, with ubiquitous reports of rape, murder, and destruction, can easily prejudice our discernment.

SUBJECTIVISM

In its extreme form, subjectivism means that individuals with opposing opinions are, in fact, both right at the same time. What this means is that there is not an external set of objective principles which regulate the veracity of statements, beliefs, or actions. According to this idea, "we place individual reason and personal experience above objective, external authorities . . . Religion must rest upon man's inner sense of right and wrong." Subjectivism "stresses 'the conversion experience' above creeds, church, ministry, and sacraments." Thus, modern man is becoming "more anti-dogmatic, skeptical of authority, and reliant upon his own religious and ethical judgments."[53] Every person is his or her own pope—objective

---

50. Keller, *"Secularization"* 69.
51. Ibid.
52. Ibid.
53. *Encyclopedic Dictionary of the Western Churches*, 732.

truth is not attainable. In some forms of subjectivism, everything depends on private interpretation; private opinion is the controlling norm. This is an aspect of contemporary culture that compounds the effects postmodernism, pluralism, and cultural individualism.

POVERTY

The number of Americans living below the poverty level has risen considerably since 2000. In some areas of the U.S., poverty has increased by 10%. The poverty level, in 2006, was defined as a family of three making less than $15,219 per year. In 2007, 37 million, or approximately 13% of Americans live below the poverty level (in the state of Texas, 23% of children live in poverty.) The economic picture, overall, is rather unsettling: President Bush's tax cuts, now extended to 2010, give a tax break of only $10 a year to those earning between $20,000 and $30,000; those with an annual income at and above one-million dollars get a tax break of $42,700. According to recent reports, 47 million Americans are uninsured—a 15% increase since 2000. Sixty-three percent of federal housing subsidies go to households earning more than $77,000; only18% go to households earning less than $16,500. Credit card late fees are now 194% higher than in 1994. Two out of every five elderly live on less than $18,000 a year, including Social Security Benefits."[54] Given these figures, it is certain that poverty is bound to increase. Our taxes are doing little to feed the hungry or clothe the naked. In the land of plenty, these numbers represent an open wound in our culture. Our social conscience appears to be non-existent, especially given the complacency that has settled over our communities. There is little sensitivity to the common good,[55] either in the government or in the public arena.

Cardinal Lecaro, during discussions in the Second Vatican Council, delivered a very impassioned speech, in which he pleaded that "the church itself must be culturally 'poor.'" He asked the "church to renounce certain riches of a glorious, but perhaps anachronistic past...because they may prevent the Church from opening itself to the true values of modern

---

54. These statistics are taken from Clara Jeffrey, "Poor Losers," Mother Jones 27 (July–August, 2006), 20.

55. For a good definition of the "common good" see Steinfels, ed., *American Catholics and Civic Engagement*, 3–18.

culture or of ancient non-Christian cultures . . ."⁵⁶ Words that can, and may yet, save us.

RATIONALISM

During the French revolution (1789–1799), the goddess of reason was enthroned on the high altar of the Cathedral of Notre Dame in Paris. It was a desecration and a protest against religious faith and institutional religion, which had been identified, by some, with the brutal power of the monarchy. The tensions between faith and reason have been part of our religious history since at least the medieval era. Rationalism "is a system of thought or attitude of mind which holds that human reason is self-sufficient and does not need the help of divine revelation to know all that is necessary for a person's well-being, also the view that a priori reason can give certitude without experience or verification of facts."⁵⁷ Thus, under rationalism, we do not need religious or any other kind of authority to tell us to arbitrate what we know to be true. Reason is self-sufficient. Historically, rationalism was the result of the de-Christianization of French society; and, although it may be a reaction to the rise of fundamentalism in our society, rationalism is making a comeback in our modern culture.

MILITARISM

The *Random House Dictionary* defines militarism as "the tendency to regard military efficiency as the supreme ideal of the State and to subordinate all other interests to those of the military."⁵⁸ In recent years, our military budget has exploded to $276, 700 billion. That is almost $23 billion *more* than China. The U.S. has, by far, the largest military budget in the world—far surpassing the next largest, and equaling the combination of the total budgets of several of the Big Eight. It has been reliably reported that the U.S. now has over 1000 military bases scattered throughout 130 foreign countries; it has another 6000 bases in the U.S. alone. The U.S. military employs 44,446 civilian officials, and subcontracts thousands of local workers, who do all the dirty work like cleaning latrines, etc. Many civilian industries, like Haliburton, Kellogg, Brown and Root, serve these far-flung bases for considerable profit. In Okinawa, the Marine Corps has

---

56. CDVII, 5: 267.
57. Hardon S.J., *Modern Catholic Dictionary*, 456.
58. *Random House Dictionary*, unabridged edition (New York: 1987), 1220.

ten bases occupying 1,186 acres. Even private companies, like Burger King, are doing rather well in and around all these military installations. The Burger King at the Baghdad Airport is one of the busiest in the world.[59] All of this is part of American imperialism.

President Dwight Eisenhower issued his famous warning in 1950:

> Every gun that is made, every warship launched, every rocket fired, signifies in the final sense a theft from those who hunger and are not fed, those who are cold and are not clothed.[60]

It was a warning about imperialism and militarism at the same time.

The paranoia and fear created by 9/11, and since exploited by the drumbeat of political rhetoric, has drastically affected our whole U.S. culture, in ways unparalleled in its history. The response employed by this amplified climate: more tanks, bombs, bombers, and armies. Daily we build higher barricades against real and *imagined* terrorist enemies. It is impossible to avoid the mantra—"support our troops"—on bumper stickers across the country, as if supporting the troops meant not questioning the policy behind military deployment. All the while, the evening news reports more deaths on the battlefields of our own making. And pundits naively ask, "why do they hate us?"

Andrew Bacevich, a Vietnam War veteran, has written a rather thorough and balanced analysis of the movement toward militarism:

> To state the matter bluntly, Americans in our own time have fallen prey to militarism, manifesting itself in a romanticized view of soldiers, a tendency to see military power as the truest measure of national greatness, and outsized expectations regarding the efficacy of force. To a degree without precedent in U.S. history, Americans have come to define the nation's strength and well-being in terms of military preparedness, military action, and fostering of (or nostalgia for) military ideals.[61]

Putting our trust in more and more bombs is the opposite of our scriptural message: "Some are strong in chariots; some, in horses; *but we are strong in the name of the Lord our God*" (Ps 20:8). Similarly, Isaiah rebukes the Israelites for putting their trust in chariots and horses rather than in Yahweh (Isa 30:16).

---

59. Murphy, *Are We Rome?*, 61.
60. Ibid., 75.
61. Bacevich, *The New American Militarism*, 2.

Unless Christians mount a prophetic protest, the response to weapons of mass destruction will be to build more, and stronger, weapons of mass destruction. The nature of our militaristic culture, with an ever-increasing arms budget and an ever-greater global reach, demonstrates the cyclical nature of an old axiom: violence breeds violence. The impulse governing our current cultural environment is the antithesis of Christ's life and message of love. Of course, we need an adequate defense to protect our people and security in an evil world, but when do we reach the point in our weapons build-up when we say enough is enough? We can only imagine what a different world this would be if even half of our military budget was devoted to peace-making.

IMPERIALISM

After a review of our far flung military bases, there can be no doubt about the dynamic of imperialism at the core of U.S. policy, and even our culture. If any readers still have doubts, they should read Cullen Murphy's fine, in-depth research in, *Are We Rome?*[62] Murphy draws a historical comparison between the ancient Roman Empire and present U.S. policy, a policy that reveals America as aspiring to be an empire. Imperialism is defined as "a policy, practice, or advocacy of extending power and dominion, especially by direct territorial acquisition or by gaining political and economic control of other areas."[63] Imperialism has been part of the history of nations, from the Assyrians, the Persians (sixth–fourth century B.C.E.), the Greeks under Alexander the Great, and the Roman Empire. One hardly needs to document the fact that today the U.S. is in the business of extending political and economic control over other countries. It does this through its political policy, its expanding military, and even through its international corporations. Traveling around the world, one can find a McDonald's in the most remote locations. Even in China, U.S. travelers can cater to their addiction to Starbucks' coffee.

Here, we are concerned with the cultural pathology in which, on account of our advanced education, democracy and high tech, we feel we are better than all other cultures. But this is at cross-purposes with our goal, for it is impossible to have true interculturation when one culture feels

---

62. Murphy, *Are We Rome?*, esp. ch. 4–5.

63. Merriam Webster, *Webster's Seventh New Collegiate Dictionary* (Chicago: Merriam Co. 1967) s.v. "Imperialism," 418.

superior to the other. When two cultures sit down at the table together for the breaking of bread, they are equal brothers and sisters. Anything less than full equality across the table will be an obstacle to any kind of interculturation. Imperialism, encouraged by our government and by our large international corporations, wounds our culture, inflicting us with a worldview that elevates wholesale our privileged culture, seen as a divine gift, over against all others. We are infected by a cultural feeling of superiority, backed up by a superiority of force (i.e., our high-tech bombers can bomb the rest of the world to smithereens). As an initial step, we need to acknowledge *our* imperialism before any real dialogue can take place.

It would be a mistake, however, to restrict our critique of U.S. imperialism to our world-wide military expansion. Imperialism involves much more, in fact, than armaments and military foreign policy; it entails economics and business practices. John Perkins has written a *New York Times* bestseller, exposing the powerful imperialistic dynamic that reigns within American corporate culture. There exists a working bond, according to Perkins, between "big corporations, international banks, and government."[64] In general, the purpose is to exploit poor countries that have rich undeveloped resources, mostly oil, for the benefit of U.S. companies. Perkins gives us a good description of its inner workings:

> The subtlety of this modern empire building puts the Roman centurions, the Spanish conquistadores, and the eighteenth- and nineteenth-century European colonial powers to shame. We EHMs (Economic Hit Men) are crafty; we learned from history. Today we do not carry swords. We do not wear armor or clothes that set us apart. In countries like Ecuador, Nigeria, and Indonesia, we dress like local schoolteachers and shop owners. In Washington and Paris, we look like government bureaucrats and bankers. We appear humble, normal. We visit project sites and stroll through impoverished villages. We profess altruism, talk with local papers about the wonderful humanitarian things we are doing. We cover the conference tables of government committees with spreadsheets and financial projections, and we lecture at Harvard Business School about the miracles of macroeconomics. We are on the record, in the open. Or so we portray ourselves and so are we accepted. It is how the system works. We seldom resort to anything

---

64. Perkins, *Confessions of an Economic Hit Man*, 94.

illegal because the system itself is built on subterfuge, and the system is by definition legitimate.[65]

The real system is, in fact, fairly complicated, but we may be familiar with some of the major players like Bechtel, Standard Oil, United Fruit, and Halliburton. The latter's connection with Dick Cheney, a former CEO of Halliburton, has often made the news since the Iraq war. We know from the newspapers that Halliburton is making unprecedented amounts of money as an unofficial arm of the government in the reconstruction of Iraq. In this case, the connection between militaristic imperialism and corporate economic imperialism is quite evident.

Another form of economic imperialism involves business-interest driven fiscal policy. One such example is the confiscatory nature of governmental loan policy in the developing world, whereby, through the World Bank, loans of enormous sums of money are given to poor, undeveloped countries; but, the loans are so large that everybody involved knows these countries can never pay them back. The U.S. government, and the multinational corporations, though, know that, instead of money, they can demand "a pound of flesh" in the form of oil, fruit, coal, labor, forests and more military bases. Thus, the poor countries are indebted to the U. S. forever, and become, in effect, part of the U.S. global empire. Rivers of natural resources extracted from developing countries through the advanced technology of U. S. corporations now flow into the U.S. on a daily basis. Sometimes just the profits, rather than the actual resources, come back to the U.S. Yes, you can buy a Big Mac in Tokyo and a Starbucks cappuccino in China. But these are only symbols of a much deeper and wider imperialism.

While it is impossible to describe in detail the inner workings of the imperialism of our U. S. 'corporatocracy,' we get strong hints here and there. For instance, even the pundits are sure we will never totally get out of Iraq. We will stay at least as long as the oil lasts, and as long as we find our presence in the Middle East beneficial to empire building in that part of the world. For our purposes, more important than the fine details is for all of us to understand our own role in the process. The real truth calls for a profound inner, and rather difficult, conversion. Perkins gets to the nitty-gritty toward the end of his shocking book:

---

65. Ibid., xxiv.

Diagnosing our Cultures' Wounds

The real story of modern empire—of the corporatocracy that exploits the desperate and is executing history's most brutal, selfish, and ultimately self-destructive resource grab—has little to do with what was exposed in the newspapers that morning and has everything to do with us. And that, of course, explains why we have such difficulty listening to the real story. We prefer to believe the myth that thousands of years of human social evolution has finally perfected the ideal economic system, rather than to face the fact that we have merely bought into a false concept and accepted it as gospel. We have convinced ourselves that all economic growth benefits humankind, and that the greater the growth, the more widespread the benefits. Finally, we have persuaded one another that the corollary to this concept is valid and morally just: that people who excel at stoking the fires of economic growth should be exalted and rewarded, while those at the fringes are available for exploitation.[66]

THE CLASH OF CULTURES

While this book tries to provide some insight into multiculturalism, and a possible Christian response, there is an urgent responsibility pressing upon us to recognize that right now we are passing through a stage of a "clash of cultures."[67] Ever since the Crusades, Muslims and the Christian West have engaged in a protracted struggle with each other. In spite of recent political rhetoric to the contrary, the West has said, in effect: "We hold you in contempt, and demonstrate this by mocking your religion and violating your deepest values." And Muslims have responded: "You, the West, are corrupt the way you live, if not diabolical...your civilization is condemned by God, who will eventually enable us to avenge ourselves on you."[68] While such sentiments may seem extreme, they reflect increasingly the reality in which we are living; but, these kinds of attitudes are hardly conducive to living together in ecumenical harmony. William Pfaff is certainly correct in concluding that "the influence of multiculturalism in the U.S. academy has not reduced the effect of more xenophobic popular attitudes, especially with respect to the Muslims."[69] This is quite

---

66. Ibid. 255.
67. William Pfaff, *"Clash of Cultures"* Commonweal, 133/13 (June 2006): 13.
68. Ibid., 14.
69. Ibid.

clearly the prevalent attitude of the West; and it does not apply only in reference to Muslims. The modern West acts like it wants to dominate all other the cultures, which it has decided are fundamentally inferior. There is little respect for the values of ancient civilizations; the belief is held that all the other cultures need to 'get with it and modernize like us.' As long as the West feels it is superior to all the other cultures, it will try to impose its form of democracy, its values, and structures upon others on the grounds that we are liberating ancient cultures from their benighted and outmoded life style.

ECOLOGY

For at least the last decade, reliable research reveals that human activity, such as driving gas-guzzling vehicles, is responsible for global warming. The Catholic Church perceives, in regard to climate change, a fundamental moral issue: "At the root of the destruction of the natural environment," wrote Pope John Paul II, "lies an anthropological error, which unfortunately is widespread in our day . . . too little effort is made to safeguard the moral conditions for an authentic 'human ecology.'"[70] Unfortunately, the most prevalent way of understanding creation, in popular forms of Christian theology, is a literal reading of the first chapter of Genesis; such an approach not only reduces the act of creation to a past event—read as six literal, twenty-four periods—but also delimits the presence and activity of God to a particular space and span of time, thus resulting in an ever-increasing tendency among Christians to ignore the *spiritual* dimension of the present, on-going created realm. The literalist approach succumbs to a dualism that dissolves the connection between God and creation; it is this dualism that is at the heart of the error seen by Pope John Paul II, and it is that which must be overcome if the *moral* imperative of a proper relationship to nature and to the world is to be understood.

If, on the other hand, we understand the creation account in Genesis to be the starting-point—that is, a *story* of God beginning creation—but not the terminal point of the act of creation, we might be able to envision creation as a continual process; this depends upon understanding the account of creation in Genesis as a story, a narrative, which is not the same as history. St. Paul, for instance, has no problem saying: "if anyone is in

---

70. Jeff Severns Guntzel, "Making Connections," *National Catholic Reporter*, 16 June 2006, 1a.

Christ, he is a *new* creation" (2 Cor 5:17). In Christ we are all participants in on-going holy creation, which is continually coming into being. This is reflected, beautifully and materially, in the way the church uses earthly material in its celebrations: oil, water, wine, and bread—these give birth to new life. With the church's sacramental system we can look at every earthly thing God has made as having the potential for being a sacrament for the Holy.

So, in view of ecology, we must roll up our sleeves and first protect, and then participate in God's continuing material creation. Creation is not so much a question of making something out of nothing, but, as St. Paul shows us, seeing everything as having the potential for becoming a new creation. Matter, herein, becomes holy every day when we protect and cultivate it for a new day, a new creation. Ecology, then, means our *partnership* with God's ongoing holy creation, a partnership in which the creation story becomes our story. We are, in fact, God's co-creators. The biblical narrative says God rested on the Sabbath, but it does not say His Sabbath rest lasted forever; God has not disengaged from His creation in order to take His rest. And, as God continues to be active in bringing creation into being and preserving it in being, so we are all called to be good stewards of the Creator's great gift to us—this beautiful, spinning little earth. And, we are all accountable to our Creator for our use of His gift.

We have a long way to go. In the U.S., our own City Recycling Center reports, "each person uses and discards two pine trees every year. Americans use 50 million tons of paper each year. Americans throw away enough aluminum to rebuild the entire U.S. commercial air fleet every three months." This kind of wasteful "human activity" is a deep wound in U.S. culture. Saving those two pine trees would be one small, but useful, step toward ending the destructive effects of global warming—for which we are all responsible. Let's hope our new cultures do some prayerful discernment before they "enculturate" into our wasteful life style.

RACISM

Martin Luther King provides the most valiant example of completely giving oneself over to the cause of racial justice and equality, even becoming a public martyr. While King's efforts brought considerable improvement, both in laws and in society, racial discrimination is still obvious and apparent in every day life. Stephen J. Pope is correct in stating that "more scandalous is the extent to which frequent churchgoers in highly Catholic places like Chicago, Boston, San Francisco, and elsewhere continue to hold racist attitudes and exhibit callous indifference to welfare recipients and immigrants."[71] All the baptized are called to offer hospitality to strangers, legal or illegal. Hurricane Katrina, in New Orleans, brought us face-to-face with the really ugly aspects of racism. Anyone watching the images that emerged from that disaster knows without a doubt that racism remains a deep wound in our culture. Those of us living near the southern border, who visit the homes of the poor immigrants, are still embarrassed to hear the discriminatory comments from fellow Catholics.

The American bishops for many years have lead the way in denouncing all forms of discrimination. Already in a 1919 Pastoral Letter the U.S. bishops condemned racism:

> In the eyes of the Church, there is no distinction of race or nation, there are only
> human souls, and these have all alike been purchased at the same price, the blood of Jesus
> Christ . . . In the name of justice and charity, we deprecate most earnestly all attempts at stirring up racial hatred."[72]

The bishops repeated that condemnation in an official statement in 1958, and again in a special statement in 1963. On November 14, 1979, the U.S. Bishops published their wonderful Pastoral Letter, *Brothers and Sisters to Us*; the letter minces no words in condemning: "every form of discrimination against individuals and groups—whether because of race, ethnicity, religion, gender, economic status, or national or cultural origin . . ." The bishops repeat emphatically the earlier statements that "racism is a sin."[73] Racial discrimination, the bishops tell us, is a "moral and religious issue;"[74] but, one has to wonder if Catholics ever confess this sin. At any rate, we cannot blame the bishops—they have not been silent.

---

71. Steinfels, ed., *American Catholics and Civic Engagement*, 38.
72. "Pastoral Letter," in *National Conference of Catholic Bishops*, 289.
73. *Pastoral Letters of the United States Catholic Bishops*, IV: 343–44.
74. Ibid, 343.

Diagnosing our Cultures' Wounds

PLURALISM

Perhaps that which is most consistently true about our society, and yet likely the most unnoticed, is pluralism. Our products come from all over the world: cars from Japan (sorry, Mr. Ford); microwaves from Thailand; phones from China; televisions from Japan or Singapore. When we need tech support for our new computer, we call an 800-number that is located in India. When we sit down for supper, we eat fish which comes frozen from the fish farms in China.

Our American culture, quite plainly, is, one might say, a pluralistic mélange. To understand this mosaic culture, we need to define the two most common forms of pluralism: first, there is religious pluralism, which seeks to affirm the interests and goals of all the varied religious groups and organizations;[75] These forms of pluralism, it should be noted, are often further subdivided into various forms of expression, for which we do not have space to review them all. In this chapter we will deal, all too briefly, with pluralism in a general way; in the next chapter we will attempt to outline a possible Christian response.

Pluralism, unlike the other '-isms' we have examined, is not a *wound* in our culture, but is a challenge we face daily. We can offer a few points on how Christians might reflect seriously on pluralism's implications for the Christian life, in order to help formulate a pastoral response to the pluralistic world in which we live. Pluralism is, in fact, the basic character of the social structure of our culture, and has been so since the early formation of our country. The history of immigration—the bedrock of our national identity—is a history of a 'plurality' of peoples and cultures who have settled this country. The waves of immigrants who arrived, especially in the nineteenth and twentieth centuries, were called by many names: squatters, settlers, and pioneers; these folks fled famine, poverty, and persecution in their home countries to find a better life here. And, in their settling, the pluralistic shape of our social fabric began. Historically speaking, then, pluralism describes our national identity. Today, in our unawareness of the pluralistic foundation of our nation's history, we struggle with the ideas of multiplicity and difference. But, as Murray notes, the strength of the identities of our communities lies in our ability to discuss

---

75. The late Fr. Jacques Dupuis S.J. wrote a hefty, and controversial, book on religious pluralism, *Toward a Christian Theology of Religious Pluralism*. Chapter 14 on "Interfaith Dialogue" is especially helpful. Fr. Dupuis himself spent 36 years teaching in India.

openly, and we have often arrived at consensus *in* multiplicity; even where we have not, we have found the capability to live with the tensions. When we recognize this strength, and when we appreciate with greater awareness our common history of plurality, we will grow more comfortable and in acceptance of pluralism in our culture. But, this is merely one aspect; as we will see in the next chapter, there are issues we need to be cognizant of in terms of *religious* pluralism.

UNBRIDLED U.S. CAPITALISM

American capitalism, with its dominant corporate mentality, has been compared to jungle life. Big corporate animals devour the small ones—other businesses, markets, and even consumers. Or, they simply step on them, squashing out their existence (think Wal-Mart.) The failures of the capitalist system are also described in a Pastoral Letter from twenty years ago by the U. S. Bishops:

- Poor and homeless people sleep in community shelters and in our church basements; the hungry lineup in soup lines.
- Unemployment gnaws at the self-respect of both middle-aged persons who have lost jobs and the young who cannot find them.
- Hardworking men and women wonder if the of the system of enterprise that helped them yesterday might destroy their jobs and their communities tomorrow.
- Families confront major new challenges: dwindling social supports for family stability; economic pressures that force both parents of young children to work outside the home; driven pace of life among the successful that can sap love and commitment; lack of hope among those who have less or nothing at all. Very different kinds of families bear different burdens of our economic system.
- Farmers face the loss of their land and way of life: young people find it difficult to choose farming as a vocation; farming communities are threatened; migrant farm workers break their backs in serf-like conditions for disgracefully low wages.[76]

The 37 million people in the U.S. living below the poverty line, as noted earlier, have continued to grow in the last 20 years. As Christians we

---

76. National Conference of Catholic Bishops, *Economic Justice for All*, in *Pastoral Letters*, 1: 397.

cannot forget the 800 million of our sisters and brothers living in absolute poverty worldwide, and the 450 million malnourished, who are facing starvation and certain death. These numbers are rarely discussed on the evening news. Perhaps the news media intentionally ignore these facts because they might bother the national conscience; or, even more troublesome, the news 'consumer' may be plainly uninterested or bored. In view of these figures, and the fact that often these conditions are the result of Western economic policy and activity, we can hardly extol capitalism as an unqualified success.

Now, we can add to the above the loss of pensions and health care for workers. The unequal distribution of wealth forms a class culture in which the rich, directly and indirectly, exploit the poor. Often, exploitation occurs with the help of the government. A recent editorial reports that "those at the very top of the nation's economic ladder have seen their income climb exponentially over the last twenty-five years. Top corporate executives now earn *three hundred times* the average way of their employers"—that's a tenfold increase for management since the 1970s.[77] In addition, the corruption of large corporations spills over into the government at the expense of American taxpayers. To contribute to the unprecedented gains of corporate profit, migrant farm workers, legal or undocumented, are being exploited, "breaking their backs in slave-like conditions for "disgracefully low wages." The unvarnished truth is that capitalism, as a system, is broken. In the next chapter we will explore what we, "the little guys," can do to fix it. And, perhaps, we can begin to heal some of the other wounds in our culture, as discussed above.

This diagnosis is, of course, incomplete. It deals only with the wounds in our culture. It does not include the many good qualities and strengths of our culture. It deals only with those parts of our culture that need healing. In this sense the diagnosis is quite limited and one-sided. But a complete diagnosis which would include the virtues and strengths, the healthy part of our cultures, would require another book, or, at least, a long chapter.

---

77. Editorial Staff, "Fairness & the Economy," *The Economist*, 22 September 2006, 5.

Healing and Developing our Multiculturalism

QUESTIONS FOR DISCUSSION

1. Which one of the wounds listed in this chapter do you feel is the most serious? Why?
2. What can you, your parish and your community do about that wound? What's the first step?
3. What wounds do you feel are missing in the long list?
4. Which one of the wounds would you like to heal first, second, third, etc.?
5. Do you ever feel like you yourself are infected by any of these wounds? Which ones?
6. Are your TV programs infected by any of the listed wounds? How? What can you do about it?
7. What can you do about consumerism? What steps can you take today?
8. Does your parish pastoral council have any committees which deal with any of the listed wounds?
9. Do you feel Vatican II went overboard in asking Christians to build a more human culture? Why?

5

Anointed to Heal our Cultures' Wounds

ONE OF THE MOST powerful symbols used throughout both the Hebrew Bible and the Christian New Testament is water. From the passage through the Reed Sea to the Lord's Baptism in the Jordan River, the biblical narratives testify to the power of water to give birth to new life (in the Jewish desert environment water was all the more precious). Even more, the fluid nature of water as a symbol is reflected in its ability to symbolize both *death* (the crushing of the Egyptians in the crashing waves of the Reed Sea) and *life* (freedom from slavery in Egypt, and birth in the waters of baptism). Water is so potent as symbol because it is a necessary feature in all forms of life.

However, we tend to forget the equally powerful symbolism of *oil* in both Testaments. Olive trees were plentiful in the Holy Land, especially in the fertile Southern Galilee, where both wild and cultivated olive trees grew to thirty-five feet tall. Accordingly, olive oil was quite abundant in this region, and played a central part in everyday life. This accounts for its frequent use, both practical and symbolic, in the scriptural narratives. One of olive oil's proscribed uses was medicinal. We see this, for instance, in the story of the Good Samaritan: "He went up and bandaged his wounds, bathing them with oil and wine" (Lk 10:34). On account of the routine medicinal employment of olive oil, the Jewish Christians would not have been surprised when James suggests: "Is anyone of you ill?" Send for the elders of the congregation to pray over him and *anoint him* with oil in the name of the Lord" (Jas 5:14).

A second purpose of anointing with oil was to make a person or thing sacred. Thus, in the Hebrew scriptures several kings—Saul, David and Solomon—are anointed with oil as part of the sacred ceremony which signifies their royal status, and the fact that they are marked out—chosen—by Yahweh. Priests are also anointed, almost bathed, with oil. In fact, the Aaronic priesthood begins with a fulsome anointing with oil: "He poured anointing oil on Aaron's head and so consecrated him" (Lev 8:12). Anointing with oil has an additional sense of power, authority and mission. Thus, in the sense of mission, we read in Isa 61:1: "The spirit of the Lord is upon me because the Lord has anointed me; he has sent me to bring good news to the humble, to bind up the broken-hearted..." In our baptism we too are anointed to bring good news, to bind up the broken-hearted, and to heal our culture's wounds. The Lord will do the healing; but He needs us to do the anointing. We are the living symbols for healing, an identity we receive in our anointing.

We can easily understand why during our baptism the priest first anoints us with oil, and only then pours the water. The baptismal oil, in the words Vatican II, consecrates us into a holy priesthood: "The baptized, by regeneration and the anointing of the Holy Spirit, are consecrated into a spiritual house and a holy priesthood." Through baptismal anointing they also "share in Christ's prophetic office."[1] But the healing power of oil is not restricted to the moment when it is applied sacramentally during baptism or the anointing of the sick. "During the patristic period," Joseph Martos tells us, "oil was indeed a sacrament of physical and spiritual health ... It was a sacrament in the broad sense, for it symbolized the healing power of the Holy Spirit, whose activity was often described as a spiritual anointing."[2] Anointed with oil and baptized with the Spirit, we are marked out—claimed—by Christ to embark on His mission of healing.

So, anointed and commissioned by Christ Himself, what are we going to do about healing our own sick culture? How are we going to be the 'yeast and salt of the earth, and the 'healing oil' for the ills of our society? Also, how do we extend the sacrament of the anointing of the sick into our own afflicted culture? Through our anointing in Christ, the healing power of Christ flows through us—symbolically and really—so that we are now the healing oil of the Holy Spirit in our communities. Anointed by the Spirit, and in union with our priests, deacons and bishops, we are commissioned to sanctify, teach, and guide our cultures, both religious and secular. By word and deed we need to anoint and heal the wounds in our culture, as described in the previous chapter. In this chapter, we will explore the

---

1. DVII, No.10.
2. *Doors to the Sacred*, 374.

possible ways in which we might be able to bring about this healing; following this, we will explore ways of developing our newly healed culture, in obedience to the mandate of Vatican II, in the next chapter.

SOME GENERAL PRINCIPLES

From the human point of view, the ideas stated above may seem to be a broad, ambitious, and, frankly, impossible agenda. The biggest mistake many of us make in setting our goals is to set our expectations too high, especially in the beginning. But, we can always start with one small step from wherever we are—this step leads to others, and, soon enough, even largest goals can be achieved. It is the first step that often seems to be the most difficult actually to make, and we often hear the complaint: "What can one person do?" Answer: A lot!

To begin with a somewhat personal example: twenty-five years ago I lived in an apartment where all kinds of cans, boxes, bottles, newspapers, and an endless variety of 'junk' was thrown daily into the garbage. Even then, I was shocked at such waste. I wondered: 'Where will all that 'junk' go, if not in our fields, rivers and streams?' I was convinced we were recklessly destroying our environment, which is God's holy creation. So, I took one small step. I wrote a simple letter to the proper department in the city suggesting a separate recycling bin be placed on our apartment grounds (recycling bins were somewhat rare in those days). I received a courteous thank-you note from the department, and in two weeks a large recycling bin was delivered to our apartment. The manager then sent a note to all the tenants reminding them to recycle. In the process, a few hundred apartment-dwellers became more conscious of the need for recycling, and gradually became more responsible stewards of God's holy creation. A wound in our culture was being healed by one small step.

Before we discuss, in more detailed form, how to heal the list of ills described in the last chapter, it may be helpful to frame our examination with some general principles: 1) Grace offered, even if rejected, is still grace. 2) One stone thrown into the water creates many ripples. 3) Like the prophets of old, we may not see any visible results in our own life time. 4) Our "mere" presence, say at a rally or protest, is a powerful witness and sacrament. After all, our anointed presence alone is 'healing oil' applied to society's wound. 5) Our letters, e-mail, or phone calls are precious tokens of dialogue. God's mighty grace, invisible to us, can, and does, pass through such 'sacramental' and conversational bonds. With this in mind, we need to recognize that the healing process often is invisible and cannot be measured in human terms. We do not judge success or failure strictly by visible, earthly standards. So, on account of this, we should not get discouraged because of 'apparent' failure.

6) We cannot say or do evil so that good may come from it. So, for instance, we cannot, through stem-cell research, kill a human embryo (evil) so that we can treat or cure illness (good). We cannot torture prisoners (evil) so that we can get information on terrorists (good). We cannot lie about racism, in the U.S., so that new cultures will feel more accepted and comfortable in our culture. They will run into our culture's racial discrimination soon enough, and the lie will be exposed for what it is. This Catholic moral principle is violated, almost daily, by our government; but the fact that the government does it routinely does not change the principle or the necessity of our adherence.

7) We cannot escape our own cultural conditioning, as it is an integral part of our personal identities. Thus, our own wounded culture is part of who we are, even as we are blessed and anointed with a call to holiness. Anointing will heal us, as baptized Christians, too. 8) Like the prophets of old, "Catholics faithful to Jesus' words and deeds, are 'resident aliens' in every society."[3] We cannot heal our culture or society if we passively accept or merely content ourselves 'to get along with' the wounded culture we are trying to anoint and heal. Therefore, we need a conversion from our insecure need to be accepted, and become something of an outsider, like the *alien*—the Good Samaritan. 9) We will feel the tension felt by the prophets themselves when we try, even by simple witness, to heal our wounded culture. And, in this, we must be cognizant that the temptation to ease that tension, by simply accepting the culture as it is, will always be with us. 10) In our everyday lives, "grounded in the security of grace, we can venture into new neighborhoods, meet strangers, and seek together to live beyond the impressed lines of history. Only through grace can we create something new."[4] Even though we cannot change anybody ourselves, the Holy Spirit can and does use us as sacraments of grace to accomplish amazing changes. We need only recall how God used Saul, a staunch enemy of Christianity, to convert the Gentile world to Christianity. The new

---

3. Steinfels, ed., *American Catholics and Civic Engagement*, 130.

4. Simone Campbell, SSS, "Beckoned by Grace" *Network Connection* 34, No. 4 (July–August, 2006): 3.

Paul suffered stoning and beatings in the process, but these became seeds for the spread of the Gospel.

11) In general, real dialogue will slowly-but-surely energize our community's healing process. What this looks like, though, is not boisterous pronouncements and exclamations on our part; dialogue is, in reality, 85% painful listening and 15% responding. And, it will be painful, because we have to die momentarily to our own opinions and our strong urge to speak. We will never speak the healing word while we are clinging tenaciously to our own "answer." Also, we know in our hearts that our healing word is not effective unless the one who is wounded is inclined to receive it. 12) We should start new coalitions, both because they are more effective and because in this prophetic ministry we all need community support. In fact, there is a great deal of power in community—politicians, even, are apt to listen to community coalitions. *Together* we can move mountains. Let us never forget Dr. Martin Luther King's 1963 'I Have a Dream' speech at the Lincoln Memorial in Washington, DC. The thousands who gathered to hear him, by their presence, planted a seed that germinated into the initial stages of healing our racist culture. 13) The healing ministry being proposed here will be difficult; at times, it will be exceedingly difficult. However, we are all called, in the words of Sr. Joan Chittister, "to live at the center of society to leaven it, at the bottom of society to speak for it, and on the edge of society to critique it."[5] To this we might add: to live in the wounded part of society to heal it.

ANOINTING AND HEALING CULTURE BEGINS

With the above principles in mind, we are ready to examine *how* we might begin to heal the wounds in our culture. It may be helpful before beginning this section, in order to refresh one's memory, to look back at the previous chapter and see the particular wounds and the definitions of which we will be exploring here. In this section, and throughout the rest of the chapters, we are taking up the process—the action.

1. Consumerism

We can actually live with Franciscan detachment without being a Franciscan. One of the first steps that we can take to combat our impulse towards consuming is to analyze what we already have. This action is two-

---

5. Chittister, *National Catholic Reporter*, 1 September 2006, 3.

fold, involving a survey and a purge: review the 'junk' in our living spaces, and then call the St. Vincent de Paul Society or the Salvation Army and simply give it away. Or better still, we can take it personally to an impoverished family who can use it, and thereby become an instrument of help to them. A small practical goal, that which can enable one to get started, is to aim to get rid of everything that was not used within the last year.

Further, we can check our shopping cart before we go to the cashier, answering honestly what we can do without; even more, we should ask ourselves what is for us, and what is for that poor family we pass on the way home? If the response to the latter inquiry is 'nothing,' we should not leave until we have something that is for them, so that we always check out with separate bags. Additionally, our buying habits can be transformed, not just in the market aisles, but also by turning off the 'buy now!' images on our television sets; or, when we buy the newspaper, take out the advertising section and throw it in the recycling bin before driving home (or clip it out and toss it in the home recycling bin if the paper is delivered). The point is that a sale should *never* be a sale if we don't really need it.

Even in the face of the onslaught of aggressive marketers we are not without options. We can join "Alternatives for Simple Living," a nonprofit group, started in 1973, which "equips people of faith to challenge consumerism, live justly and celebrate responsibly."[6] Or, we can declare our very own "Buy Nothing Day," along with the thousands who celebrate such a day on 'Black Friday,' the frenzied shopping day after Thanksgiving. There is also the option to join "Clutterless Recovery Groups, Inc." founded by Mike Nelson, the author of *Stop Clutter from Wrecking your Family*.[7] If there is no St. Vincent de Paul Society in your parish, you can join Heifer International.[8] This is one of the favorite charities of The Bill & Linda Gates Foundation. In joining this group, you will also be helping to sponsor their efforts to end hunger and poverty in East Africa. Through very simple steps, we can heal the wound of our pervasive consumerism by starting with our own lives.

2. Racism

Racism is one of our culture's deepest wounds. This is where whitewash and cover-up abound at all levels in our society. It took a violent hurricane

---

6. As per the group's website, see www.simpleliving.net
7. Mike Nelson, *Stop Clutter from Wrecking your Family*. www.clutterless.org.
8. Heifer International, 1 World Ave. Little Rock, AR 72202.

just to give us a passing glimpse under and behind all that whitewash. Only God knows how much more of the same exists as a hidden leprosy within our culture. In the face of it all, we need a large dose of courage, patience and faith in the power of grace. "Fight the good fight of the faith," St. Paul reminds us (1 Tim 6:12). "Racism," writes Ruth Benedict, "is an '-ism' to which everyone in the world today is exposed; for or against we must take sides. And the history of the future will differ according to the decision which we make."[9]

The healing actions we can apply to anoint the wounds of racism are almost endless. They are limited only by our own imaginations. As a business owner one can make the deliberate choice to hire minority candidates; as neighbors we can perform acts of hospitality—a carpool to the market; an always open invitation to meals; cutting the lawn of our neighbor when we cut our own. We can visit the minority families who have moved into our neighborhoods, and welcome them with genuine Christian Hospitality. As members of bread-breaking communities, we could well show our Christian hospitality by inviting them to our house to break bread with us at a welcoming dinner. Our position on racism must be open and public—we can quote the American Bishops: "Racism is a *sin*."

3. Abortion

The Church has struggled with this issue for many centuries, going all the back to the very early years of the Church. The *Didache*, or *The Teaching of the Twelve Apostles* (c. 140 A.D.), states clearly: "You shall not procure abortion, nor destroy a new-born child."[10] A century-and-a-half later, the Council of Elvira (c. 300) decreed: "If a woman, in the absence of her husband, has conceived in adultery, and has killed that which came of her deed, it is determined that she is not to be given communion even at death . . . "[11] But the Church's struggle has become more difficult in modern times, where abortions have increased on account of legalization; our culture has legitimated this crime under the guises of right to privacy and freedom of choice, enabled by the rejection of absolute norms. On account

---

9. Quoted by Sara Catania in "A is for Afro," *Mother Jones*, 31 (September-October 2006): 75.

10. Jurgens, *The Faith of the Early Fathers*, 2.

11. Ibid., 257.

of this, healing this cultural wound by inculcating a respect and reverence for life will require a strong prophetic stand against our culture.

We are not without help or resources in this matter. One crucial action we can perform is to begin a dialogue with those women contemplating abortion, and we should offer to help find an adoption agency. Local pro-life organizations are important resources, and one can begin to spread a positive message through pro-life bumper stickers and T-shirts. Churches, as well, can be centers of healing action, offering counseling, assistance services, and spiritual direction. And, above all, we should not narrow the category of 'pro-life' to abortion: it must include euthanasia, assisted suicide, and the death penalty. Even the most hardened criminal is, by God's grace, capable of repentance. Reliable research reveals that the death penalty is not an effective deterrent, because people who contemplate a crime are always convinced *they* will not get caught. Besides, life, in any form whatsoever, is sacred. This includes prisoners, the elderly in nursing homes, and the soldiers on the battlefield. When life is no longer sacred, we are all diminished in value before each other and before God.

4. Individualism

Individualism is a disease that inflicts our whole culture. It contradicts the law of nature, which says that we are social animals and that we need community for our very survival. Our desire for independence simply has to give way to the absolute truth that we need each other. St. Paul says it best: "As it is there are many parts, yet one body. The eye cannot say to the hand, 'I have no need of you,' nor again the head to the feet, 'I have no need of you'" (1 Cor 12:21). For, "all the members of the body, though many, are one body" (1 Cor 12:12). This social principle is inscribed upon the very heart of our Catholic faith—it is the ebb and flow of the life of the whole Church. But even more, it is the human glue that keeps society together, and keeps it functioning through unity. Christians, as committed disciples, kindle their energies to build community from morning to night. Anything less is a betrayal of the meaning of our Eucharistic bread-breaking celebration. Building community is the core identity of ministry. Community just is who we are and how we are as Church.

So what kinds of actions follow from the principle of community? For starters, we can make a point of not doing alone what can be done as a team or with others. There are many simple, small things, tasks that we often perform alone, which can—and should—be done inclusively: we can share a ride to work, or make meals together. Our lives, as persons in communities, are meant to be open and shared; we can do this simply through such things as listening to the pain of our brothers and sister in the nursing homes, hospitals, or prisons. We can learn to ask for help, to 'bother' our neighbors, when the task ahead is too much for our age or health. Building community is part of normal life, and heals society of the proud tendency 'to go it alone.' At its core, individualism is divisive—it fragments society, separating the "hand from the foot." No society can long survive when it breaks apart into selfish, inward-turning islands.

5. Relativism

In the U.S., the red traffic light has an unmistakable meaning—stop! Although a red-light may have other connotations in different cultures and societies, it is certain that traffic control of some kind is an absolute rule observed throughout the civilized world. In light of this, it is plain that every society has need of some norms or regulations that everyone within that culture recognizes and respects. For instance, all societies have a police force, or some kind of security organization, to regulate and enforce order for the sake of the safety of others. Relativism, though, in certain forms, de-legitimizes these structures; the result is that civilized life is reduced to a world without order or structure –there are no boundaries because there are no rules that qualify as absolute or can be applied to all equally. But what does this look like practically speaking? Think about the consequences of a completely deregulated business industry: the economic giant corporations free to exploit the poor without consequences. To some degree that is already happening with Wal-mart—when Wal-Mart moves in, the rest of the stores in the area close shop. Relativism in the market place can be disguised as normal competition.

6. Empiricism as an Absolute

The concept that human experience is the only, and absolute, way to knowledge easily can be shown to be internally contradictory through a few routine examples. In our everyday life, we trust doctors to treat diseases that they have never had (has every oncologist 'experienced' cancer for him or herself?); we trust lawyers to apply the law correctly, even though they have not committed any crime. In other words, every day we rely on the knowledge of others, which has been acquired largely through education, training, and professional research. On a personal level, we make serious decisions in a similar manner; and, even small children who have no experience learn about the errors of history. We can heal the wound of absolute empiricism through dialogue based upon common reflection from everyday life. In fact, our life in community would be impossible without the absolutes we take for granted—those absolutes which we do not have to experience ourselves to know they are true: Thou shalt not kill; thou shalt not steal; thou shalt not lie; thou shalt not commit adultery; thou shalt respect thy neighbors property; thou shalt keep your contracts, written or verbal.

7. Ecology

It has rightly been said that ecology is at the heart of Christian faith.[12] Environmental issues are now so serious that we need to start yesterday to pay attention to all the issues: recycling, car emissions, and air and water pollution. According to recent reports, "there are 19,533 pesticide products currently on the market . . . no data whatsoever are available for seventy percent of commercial chemicals . . . these have not been tested for health effects."[13] That is just a glimpse of a growing world-wide problem. We who are called to be builders and sacraments of healing are in reality destroying our beautiful planet that is the site of God's creation. There is a great onus for us to realize that there is no other—if we destroy this one we destroy ourselves. We simply have to heal and save the planet we have and share now.

For Christians, the first step has to be an *ecological conversion*. This involves a complete change of attitude! We need the inner motivation that will sustain our efforts day and night, especially when the task seems impossible. There can be no doubt that our ongoing pollution of God's holy creation is a serious moral issue. Here, all Christians have a vocation and responsibility to lead the culture and, like the prophets of old, to sting the world's conscience by word and example.

The creation story reminds us of the vocation of all humans: "The Lord God took the man [Adam = symbol for humanity] and settled him in the Garden of Eden, *to cultivate and care for it*" (Gen 2:15). So, even in

---

12. See Denis Edwards, *Ecology at the Heart of Faith*.
13. Bullard, *The Quest for Environmental Justice*, 214.

the Garden of Eden we were not destined to sit in our Lazy-boy and watch the sun go down; rather, we were called to be *partners* with our Creator in cultivating and caring for the gift of creation. It is clear that "human beings have a unique moral responsibility for other creatures. There is a unique moral demand made upon them to respond urgently, creatively, and wisely to the ecological crisis they have created."[14]

Our Jewish brothers and sisters have a wonderful phrase, *Tikkum Olam*, which means 'repairing the world.' This prayerful intonation "represents the continuing obligation to make God's mercy and love visible throughout the world."[15] It also expresses the fact that God's created world is in constant need of repair—redemption is not complete without the healing of the world. With all the floods, hurricanes, tornadoes and earthquakes, we know the world is not perfect—the task given to us by the Creator is to be sacraments of healing in a broken world. For Jews and for Christians, 'repairing the world' is an ethical responsibility with roots in the First Covenant. We are God's partners in the continuing creation of the world.

There is an additional surplus of hope, for Christians, in the new covenant of Christ. Because Christ redeems and reconciles all things to himself (Col 1:20) Christians know that all of creation is precious. There is no animal, no bird, no insect, and no fish that is beyond God's infinite love. Denis Edwards tells us that even "each sparrow participates in redemption in Christ."[16] Jesus Christ, who shed His blood and rose again, brings into being new creation: "We know that the whole creation has been groaning in travail together until now" (Rom 8:22).

Our own contribution to realizing creation takes place in everyday tasks. For starters, we can pick up the empty, discarded cans on our own street and add them to our empty soup cans in our recycling bins, or on the way to the recycling center. Also, our consumer choices, even small ones, can have an impact: for instance, buy Yuban Coffee, which is committed to conserving the environment and the wildlife in coffee-growing regions.[17] Small steps of activism can be employed, by writing our

14. Edwards, *Ecology at the Heart of Faith*, 22.

15. John Pawlikowski, "The Challenge of *Tikkum Olam* for Jews and Christians," in *Seeing Judaism Anew*, 227.

16. Edwards, *Ecology at the Heart of Faith*. 95.

17. Yuban Coffee has the following ad: "Yuban is the world's largest supporter of Rainforest Alliance Certified coffee beans. This partnership protects the environment

Senators and Representatives about supporting anti-pollution laws. At our local churches, we can remind our fellow workers and parishioners at the parish festival about our stewardship of God's holy creation; and, we can conduct an adult education course at our parish on ecology. With its visibility in popular culture, we could show the documentary film by Al Gore entitled: *An Inconvenient Truth*. After the film we could conduct small group discussions on what we, as co-creators of this earth, can do as a parish. In our homes, we can declare our very own Earth Day: bike to work, plant a tree, replace all the light bulbs in the house. But, whatever you do, invite a friend to help you, as that is how we spread the word and involves others (i.e., raising their awareness). Esme Floyd, who published the most practical book on the market today about these issues, proves that saving our planet begins in our own home with our very own life style.[18]

We are accountable to our Creator for the use of His gift of creation, and for the way we live and act as partners of His continuing creation. We show respect and reverence for His gift, not by trampling over it or destroying it, but by healing it where it is wounded, and by nourishing it to new life where it is dying. Created nature, after all, is a holy, living picture of the Creator. God, the supreme artist, is present in all of His works. That is why we sing and pray with all of creation during our Sunday morning liturgies:

> Bless the Lord all you works of the Lord,
> praise and exalt him above all forever ...
> Sun and moon, bless the Lord ...
> Every shower and dew, bless the Lord ...
> Ice and snow, bless the Lord ...
> You springs, bless the Lord;
> Seas and rivers, bless the Lord ...
> Mountains and hills, bless the Lord ...
> All you beasts, wild and tame, bless the Lord.
> Blessed are you in the firmament of heaven.
> Praiseworthy and glorious forever.[19]

8. Unbridled capitalism

A power we all have is the power of the boycott. We can refuse to buy the products of those companies who do not pay a living wage, who

---

and supports the people and wildlife in coffee growing regions."

18. Floyd, *1001 Ways to Save our Planet*.
19. From the *Benedicte, omnia opera*.

Anointed to Heal our Cultures' Wounds

discriminate against women, African-Americans, or other minorities. Often we will need to do our own research, or ask the workers at Target, K-mart, etc., about discrimination in wages, promotions, and benefits. We can choose where to buy gas, etc. An active boycott also necessarily involves a letter to the owner and manager. Together we can put a bridle on capitalism. As workers, we can organize or join unions, which has been recommended by many popes for well over a century. We can go to board meetings and raise questions about bidding for contracts. Also, in the age of explosive profit margins, we can call the attention of the public to the outrageous salaries paid to CEOs of corporations—salaries and packages in exponential excess to the wages of employees. Given that workers in this country are without insurance coverage, and hundreds of millions of people around the globe are without even basic care, we can write letters to Merck, etc. and ask them what they are doing, in terms of cheaper drugs, for the American public and for the victims of AIDS and other diseases through the developing world.

With these small actions, one can begin the process of change; however, one must *recognize* the need for change in this system. First, we have to be convinced that a capitalist system, which leaves 38 million in poverty in this country, and hundreds millions around the globe, and is system that is fixed so the rich get richer and the poor get poorer, is indeed broken. How we fix it is largely up to our own ingenuity and power with governing entities, both national and local. An important part of this is the need to help our senators and congressional representatives to develop a global consciousness. What harm do NAFTA and CAFTA perpetuate upon the poor in Mexico and Guatemala? What is the difference between *free* trade and *fair* trade? In the face of large U.S. monopolies and corporations is Mexico ever really free?

9. Human Sexuality

All Christians know that the bible presents sex as created by an all-holy God for a holy purpose. But, we need very badly to develop a *positive theology* about the body and human sexuality; then, we need to teach it in language all people can understand. The late Pope John Paul II gave us a good start with his theology of the body; we need to build on this resource in the recognition that there is yet a long way to go. After the Incarnation and Resurrection, the human body, including our gender and sexual function, is a 'temple of the Holy Spirit.' In light of this, as we do not profane temples, synagogues, or other holy places, so we do not profane the body. The body shares in the holy bread of the Lord at communion: our bodies are the Lord's sanctuary. They deserve the same reverence we give to "the Holy" wherever we find it. But when all is said and done, all of us, male and female, need to bend our energies to develop a real, positive theology of human sexuality. Our traditional negative policy will not do in our sex saturated culture - it has no healing power.

10. The Political Order

America's experiment in democracy is young and vulnerable. It can easily turn into an oligarchy of the rich and well connected, which sometimes appears as if that is happening. In spite of regular elections, democracy can lose its sense of accountability and fall into corruption: it can become twisted and simply "follow the money." In our current situation, it is dire that we lose the sense that the American political system is pristine or divinely ordained. That it is not is reflected, for instance, in the contradiction between the mandates of Christ for care for the poor and the fact that the poor have no lobby—no representation!—in Congress. So, all citizens need to be aware of what is at stake, not only during elections, but also during all sessions of Congress. It is a common maxim that we are a nation of laws, but not all laws are just. The quest for that justice which is beyond human laws must continue day and night. We have to rise above mere legalism, and elect legislators who have compassion, and a vision about the whole nation and the whole world. Peace-making is every Christian's vocation. And that means more than passing laws.

11. The Role of Women

Child-bearing is, of course, a critical role for any culture. But it hardly exhausts the many talents of women in our society; in fact, the net effect of such thinking is to reduce the nature and uniqueness of a person to a function. Women, as persons in society, are valuable because of who they are; and each person has unique talents and abilities to lend for the common good. Leadership roles have to be earned, either by hard work or by developed charisma. A specific gender does not automatically entitle us to leadership *in any level of society*—civil or religious. The whole of culture suffers when leadership qualities of either gender are not recognized, or when persons

Anointed to Heal our Cultures' Wounds

are deliberately passed over due to their gender on account of institutional customs, or discriminatory civil or ecclesiastical laws. Patriarchal notions of gender held over from ancient cultures, whether maintained in the churches or in civil society, is still a deep wound in modern society. The misogyny described in the last chapter, perhaps the world's oldest prejudice, is still very real in most cultures. And, given our own history and the continual growth of the presence of many cultures in our society, patriarchy and misogyny will be continual pressures we have to face.

How do we heal this wound? Most immediately, we need to vote for qualified women whenever possible—not just because they are women, but because they are qualified. Women should be promoted to leadership roles especially in areas where male prejudice persists. In all areas, across the board, the talents and skills of women must be affirmed and recognized. While upholding the priority of family life, wives and husbands need to partner together so that their contributions may be expressed fully and equally in all areas—domestic and otherwise. There are no limitations to achievement, except those we impose on each other; this is reflected, for example, in the realm of the academy, where women excel in advanced education in equal degree to, if not surpassing, their male counterparts. In the workaday world, we know that discrimination often begins in the job market. It is especially in this arena where all of us —male and female—need to apply our energies and influence. In the next chapter, we will see how both men and women can cooperate to develop and refine our cultures.

There are, of course, other wounds in our culture that need to be anointed and healed. But these few we have discussed may provide examples which we can apply to the other unnamed wounds. Our culture can be healed. We are God's nurses, doctors, therapists, and healing oil. The God who created us, and our wounded, but beautiful, world, remains the Healer.

QUESTIONS FOR DISCUSSION

1. In the "Proper Development of Culture" how do we determine what is "Proper?"
2. In reading this chapter did any part of you feel Christians should stay in the church and let the folks in the public arena take care of

the development of culture? Shouldn't we observe a wall of separation between the sacred and the secular? Why or why not?

3. Do you feel this chapter stretches our baptismal anointing a little too far? Perhaps especially for the laity? Why?

4. Can you give some examples of "repairing the world?"

5. How do we as Christians respond to women's inequality in our patriarchal culture?

6. How do we go about "peacemaking" in our community?

6

Developing our Cultures

Plato, the Greek philosopher (427–347 BCE), is famous for his dialogues, the most notable being the *Republic* and the *Crito*. Quoting Socrates, which Plato often does in his dialogues, he explains that the "the State arises out of the needs of mankind; no one is self-sufficing, but all of us have many wants." Here, Plato describes the state as a community of farmers, weavers, merchants, shoemakers, etc. "Yet," he concludes, "until the refinements of culture have been added, this is no better than a 'city of pigs.'"[1]

St. Augustine, relying on Plato's Greek philosophy, wrote his classic, *City of God* (427 CE) He writes about two cities, "created by two kinds of love: the earthly city was created by self-love reaching to the point of contempt for God, the Heavenly City by the love of God carried as far as contempt of self. In fact, the earthly city glories in itself, the Heavenly City glories in the Lord."[2] While the two cities are wholly distinct in their origin and natures, for Augustine, they overlap—their boundaries not quite distinguishable—in the course of history. Augustine's theology clearly reflects and develops the traditional teaching of the Church on original sin; in this volume, it is Augustine's argument that we are all, originally, citizens of the 'earthly city,' in that we come into the world already guilty. Corollary to this, we will never develop a perfect culture free from sin and its effects—that is the end point of the arrival of the true city of God. Nevertheless, with the aid of grace, we can always improve what we have.

When Vatican II calls us to "Proper Development of Culture," the bishops are not unaware of the sinful human condition. Nevertheless, they call us to "refine and unfold humankind's manifold spiritual and

---

1. Quoted by Daniel J. Boorstin, *The Seekers*, 45.
2. St. Augustine, *City of God*, trans. Henry Bettenson, 593.

bodily qualities ... to improve customs and institutions, to render *social life more human both within the family and in the civic community*."³ The bishops are calling us both to refine and to develop our cultures. To "refine" means to free the culture from impurities—to improve, perfect, and polish it. To "develop" means to advance, build up, fix up, and shape. With this commission, we are called to an ambitious undertaking. From the human point of view such a task may seem impossible; however, no doubt, the bishops assume that all the baptized have the grace of the Holy Spirit, which perfects the human and assists us in this ambitious undertaking.

The bishops did not provide us with a specific agenda. In refusing to spell out the details and specificities, they left open the space for us to figure out what is most crucial and how best to proceed at the local level through prayerful discernment. What follows is my own attempt to stimulate that discernment process with suggestions which grow out of the Catholic tradition, broadly understood. Our basic sources will be the documents of Vatican II, papal encyclicals, and the revised Catechism. However, there is no attempt to be complete or to place limits on the variety of ways we can refine and develop our cultures. The call of Vatican II is a call to creativity at the grassroots.

DIALOGUE

To start this process we can initiate and promote certain dynamics, movements, and activities that by their very nature will build up and develop what is truly human in our cultures. The first, and the most powerful of these dynamics, will be real dialogue. Our form of dialogue will require more listening than speaking, both within our own culture and across today's many different cultures. The more our cultures are bombarded with the noise and shouting of the media, the more difficult true dialogue will become. Dialogue, which comes from two Greek words, *dia* (through) and *logos*, (word) refers to a word process that "gets through" to the mind and heart of the other person. The process assumes the word, when sent, will be received. If not received, there is no dialogue, no matter the volume of words. This kind of dialogue cannot happen during the distractions, noise, and shouting of the mass media—television, radios and cell phones—that often controls our attention. Under these conditions, our words will never get through.

3. DVII, No. 53. [Italics mine].

Developing our Cultures

But continuing real dialogue will put us in the good company of two famous Greek philosophers: Socrates and Plato. For Socrates, dialogue is "the spoken word, the encounter between living people, with the word as the catalyst of thought that struck sparks."[4] Of course, these ancient dialogues happened before the arrival of today's print and visual cultures. Today people no longer go to the public square to talk shop, or listen to a speaker on his/her soapbox. In our contemporary culture we are all too busy to hear each other. Our culture is missing an important dimension, oral communication i.e. dialogue, and the practice of listening. Besides that, our televisions and radios reduce our public discourse to the lowest common denominator, often proceeding on a level not higher than that of a sixth grader. Meanwhile, oldsters, bored with TV fare, discuss their aches and pains, but little else.

What might true dialogue look like? Diagnostically, we should ask ourselves the following kinds of questions: when did we last invite a Muslim to dinner? When did we last have a serious, adult discussion about campaign issues during elections? When did we last visit the new neighbors on our block? With these in mind, some practical ways to initiate the process of dialogue would involve, for instance, introducing and expanding public listening sessions; initiating or attending open parish forums. Also, it is vital that we participate in whatever consultative processes come our way. The net effect of engaging in these kind of activities is the creation of mutual understanding and communal peace, for different cultures will not contend or be acrimonious with each other as long as they engage in true dialogue. Without giving up our own culture, we need to get inside of—seek to understand—the culture of our neighbor when we enter into dialogue.

THE ARTS

A vital necessity in culture is to "cultivate and care for" the arts in whatever way we can. Mozart and Beethoven, with their classical compositions, have done more to refine the cultures of the ages than all of the senators, presidents, and politicians. Even dictators, like Joseph Stalin, recognized the power of music—so much so, that he tried to suppress it.

The stained glass windows of churches and cathedrals have raised people's minds and hearts to the higher realities of life. Still today, they

---

4. Boorstin, *The Seekers*, 23.

rescue us from the drudgery of the daily grind, calling us to a state of reflection and contemplation. The Statue of Liberty, an icon of our national landscape, has the power to make hearts beat for freedom and idealism. Even cartoonists, of all persuasions, make us think; today, these panels of images can cross the globe in an instant. The power of inked illustrations lies in their ability to by-pass the limitations of spoken language, being 'read' across cultures. Works of visual art, such as the paintings of da Vinci, continue to inspire people all over the world. True art has the power to develop and refine our cultures, precisely by drawing us together and uniting in ways that eclipse mere words.

ACCOUNTABILITY

We can encourage, and, indeed, demand accountability within our communities. Accountability is the bond that keeps the community and the culture together. It is a virtue that proclaims that we are all servants to one another, and that we are answerable to each other. In the Christian faith, accountability is part of who we are as creatures under the Lordship of Christ—only the Lord is the Master. On a basic level, accountability begins in the home, and then spreads through the community; and, from there, through all forms of government, civil or ecclesiastical. Secrecy, theft, and corruption cannot survive where accountability is practiced on a daily basis. Thus, we can build a culture that strives to be free from corruption if we build upon a foundation of accountability to one another. Paul instructs us, in this wise, that we are to "take no part in the unfruitful works of darkness, but instead expose them" (Eph 5:11).

In an age of scandal, we can also commend the media when they hold public officials accountable for their service to their fellow citizens. As social animals we have responsibilities to our society at all levels. When our government passes unjust laws, we have to voice our opposition with all the powers at our command. Sometimes a rally or public protest, political or not, is the only way to make our voices heard.

We are accountable not only to each other, but also to the God of Mt. Sinai, who "inscribed the stone tablets with His own finger." Accountability, to be complete, always has both vertical and horizontal dimensions. Mt. Sinai—the Decalogue—will never become obsolete. And, we should hasten to say, this is not limited to one religion; rather, it extends to all of God's creation. These precepts will always remain the absolute and unchanging reference point for all accountability. A refined culture will always have a stable moral foundation. The command—the revelation—of God, not more bombs or guns, is the primary source of a culture's peace and security.

PEACEMAKING

Church pulpits have, for many centuries, proclaimed: "Blest are the peacemakers" (Matt 5:9). Yet, our history is stained with blood from so many wars. Contrary to the spirit of domination, in a refined and developed culture humans do not kill fellow humans. We must continue to proclaim this message from the housetops. And, giving feet to this proclamation, we can also join *Pax Christi* and other groups, who gather together to shout: 'Make peace, not war.' At this writing, there are at least 350 peacemaking groups in the U.S., including the Hip-Hop Caucus.[5] Many of these groups are sponsored by churches of various denominations, and organize non-violent, civil protests across the country. It is crucial to recognize, in all of this, that peace does not just happen—*we* have to make it happen. And we have to do it everyday. We are not surprised, therefore, that the American Bishops in 1988 named their pastoral letter, "Building Peace: A Pastoral Reflection on the Response to *The Challenge of Peace*." In this letter, they give six suggestions for building a Peacemaking Church:

1) A *peacemaking church* needs to pray constantly for peace.
2) A *church of peacemaking* is also a community which regularly shares the church's teaching on peace in its schools, religious education efforts, and other parish activities.
3) We especially need to work toward a more fully developed theology of peace.
4) A *church of peacemaking* is a community which speaks and acts for peace, a church which consistently raises fundamental moral questions about the policies that guide the arsenals of the world.
5) The voice of a *peacemaking church* must reflect the facts, rest on competent analysis and understand that persons of goodwill sometimes differ on specific questions.

---

5. For more information see www.declarationofpeace.org.

6) Finally, a *peacemaking church* is a community which keeps hope alive.[6]

The billions of dollars of our tax money allocated to killing fellow humans could be used for peacemaking, for building programs for the poor, for improving education, etc. A culture at war, or preparing for war, is not a refined or developed culture. We humans now have the awesome power to destroy God's holy creation, either by a nuclear war, or by creating a polluted environment that will make human life impossible. But, we also have the power to end all wars, and to create for ourselves a new, wholesome environment. The choice is up to us, first as individuals, then as a community.

EDUCATION

Articles 60 and 61 of the *Pastoral Constitution* are devoted to education. "The possibility now exists," the *Constitution* tells us, "of liberating most men from the misery of ignorance. Hence it is a duty most befitting our times that men, especially Christians, should work strenuously on behalf of certain decisions which must be made in the economic and political fields, both nationally and internationally."[7] The *Pastoral Constitution* goes on to say that "efforts must be made to see that men who are capable of higher studies can pursue them." Additionally, "everyone should acknowledge and favor the proper and necessary participation of women in cultural life."[8]

We need to hold both politicians and educators, private and public, accountable for providing quality education at all levels, especially to the poor. This task will not be easy, but school board meetings and parent-teachers meetings, while time consuming, are minimum steps toward improving our whole educational system. We can surely encourage greater availability of scholarship money so that the poor may be able to attend college. And, higher education must be held accountable for providing a quality education that includes the need for discipline and the teaching of moral norms. Culture cannot survive without a firm point of reference for acceptable behavior; education, then, is more than the transfer of

6 *Pastoral Letters of the United States Catholic Bishops,* V: 660–61.

7. DVII, No. 60.

8. Ibid.

knowledge and data, but the formation and shaping of individuals to be members of communities and society. Education, though, and particularly moral education, is not solely the domain of our institutions of learning; the home is the first school. But, it is equally vital that the morals and values first learned in the home and religious institutions be supported and built upon during the critical years in the classrooms, where teachers are instrumental, in addition to parents, in the delicate art of leading children to mature knowledge and responsible adult behavior.

RESEARCH

Many of the bishops' speeches, during the discussions on the *Pastoral Constitution*, stressed the need for freedom to do scientific research. It was argued that "the Council must make a special and explicit declaration about the full liberty and autonomy of scientific research when carried out wisely."[9] Article 59, of the final text of the *Constitution*, goes on at some length to describe the need for this freedom to do research. A developing culture is not static but creative and dynamic, and it must always be in the mode of discovery. This freedom of research and discovery is underwritten by the firm stance that, according to the *Constitution*, there is no conflict between science and religion. God is the author of truth wherever and in whatever form it is found. Based upon this, article 62 recommends that professors of theology "collaborate with [scholars] well versed in the other sciences."[10] In our age of specialization, good research requires such collaboration, otherwise research scholars will become so specialized that they will no longer be able to speak to each other.

Of course, research has its moral boundaries. We cannot, in the name of research, kill human life in order to save or improve it. Otherwise, we become, in the words of Plato, "no better than a city of pigs." All human life, in whatever stage, has equal value. Honoring and respecting that human life is the first step in developing our cultures. Quite plainly, we do not "make the human more human" by killing it. Our research, then, with this qualification, is about improving our lives in community.

---

9. CDVII, 269.
10. DVII, No. 62.

BUILDING COMMUNITY

Perhaps the toughest challenge in our individualistic culture is the Christian vocation to build community. Our relative affluence, and thus our independence, does not help this effort. In the Catholic system, our mega-parishes, due to the shortage of priests, are a new obstacle to community (it is no wonder that Plato, in his book of *Laws*, limits the ideal community to no more than 5,040 households). However, in spite of the obstacles, the shape of Christian of life just is communal—it is structured constitutively around the notion of community. Most centrally, Christian life *is* Eucharistic: every time we gather around our common table to break the bread of the Lord, and share it with each other, we renew our commitment to build community.

Given this fundamental vision, Christians have the resources and means at their disposal to undertake this task, even though building community across diverse ethnic and cultural communities will be an especially difficult challenge. However, we need only look to the Jesuit Volunteers, who have been engaged in such efforts for over 50 years. The Jesuits have proven that most difficulties, including the language barrier, can be overcome. The presence of the Jesuits, their compassion, shared prayer, Christian hospitality, and their continuing care become the language that builds the lasting bonds of community. Various colors, dress, and customs are earthly symbols of the rainbow of diversity our infinite God has created. These symbols most especially reveal their beauty when gathered in community worshiping the same Creator. The Jesuit Volunteers serve as saintly examples for the rest of us—community is our common goal. We are reminded of this—weekly, even perhaps daily—in the recitation of the Apostles' Creed, in which we profess the "communion of saints." Our culture remains wounded until we achieve the communion of saints in which believe.

FREEDOM

The *Pastoral Constitution*, in article 59, draws our attention to the theme "that culture has a constant need of a just freedom if it is to develop."[11] The text specifies this idea even more a few lines later: ". . . a man is free to search for the truth, voice his mind, and publicize it; that he be free to practice any art he chooses; and finally, that he have appropriate access

---

11. DVII, No. 59.

Developing our Cultures

to information about public affairs."[12] Freedom is always freedom within limits. Those limits are defined by divine and just human laws and by the needs of the common good. But we know that we grow toward maturity by the choices we make in freedom not by coercion. No. 59 forcefully "affirms the legitimate autonomy of human culture and especially of the sciences."[13] Freedom of the will is the Creator's gift to all of us. It's up to us to protect and develop that precious gift.

THE SEARCH FOR TRUTH

That the *Pastoral Constitution* (No. 62) should support a cooperative search for the truth may seem rather revolutionary. "May the faithful," states the *Constitution* "blend modern science and its theories and the understandings of most recent discoveries with Christian morality and doctrine."[14] Before Vatican II, many Catholics thought that the Church and the Church alone possessed the truth—all others were outside of the truth and thought to be destined for hell (though the Church did allow for inculpable ignorance). No one in the Catholic Church believed, then, that we still had to search for the truth, and especially not in cooperation with those outside of the Church.

Quite pertinent here is the work of Cardinal Colombo, a respected leader during the Second Vatican Council. He writes:

> ... that the possession of truth in the Church is not something dead, rigid, static, not a reason for comfortable repose, but a ceaseless, inexhaustible search, struggle and endeavor for renewal ... the truth which the church possesses is transcendent and consequently demands to be more deeply grasped and concretely applied ... it can never be exhausted in its further development."[15]

The Cardinal's words need to be understood in the context of a pre-conciliar, triumphant Church, which was convinced it alone had the monopoly on infallible truth. In view of those times, one almost has to believe that the Holy Spirit inspired Cardinal Colombo with a true Pentecostal outburst—with true prophetic discernment. His statement goes to the very heart of our continuing quest, both in theology and in

---

12. Ibid.
13. Ibid.
14. Ibid., No. 62.
15. CDVII, 284.

the secular sciences. While the Cardinal's words apply primarily to the truths possessed by the Church, this article of the *Constitution* clearly extends the cooperative search for truth to *all* of humankind, without a predetermined boundary.

That truth is not "dead, rigid, or static," is one of the great pronouncements of the *Pastoral Constitution*. The bishops at the Council, during their seminary days, had studied the "perennial" theology of the Latin textbooks, which had gone centuries without revision. Since Latin was a "dead" language, it was an appropriate vehicle to pass on the Church's unchangeable truths from one generation to the next. There was the great temptation simply to memorize these "static" truths and to repeat them routinely until death. All that changed with the *Pastoral Constitution*.

LANGUAGE

All cultures are constituted by much more than their spoken or written languages; in addition to language, cultures consist of customs, rituals, styles of life, and beliefs. The ancient Greeks, for example, had many gods and goddesses. However, they had one, called Hermes, who was a messenger and herald for all the other gods and goddesses. The main job of Hermes was to be an interpreter, an intermediary, between the gods and humans. Our English word, "hermeneutics," which is the science of interpretation, is derived from the name of this Greek god. The key insight of the Greek myth of Hermes is that it is an ancient witness that language is not self-interpreting, and that interpretation is an important part of language and communication. Dialogue between one human and another is one level of communication; but, dialogue between the gods and humans is quite another. Any communication between the divine and human worlds requires considerable interpretation.

A culture's language includes not only its words, spoken or written, but also its art, gifts, signs, symbols, customs, and celebrations. There is almost no limit in any culture to the many ways humans communicate with their deity, their fellow humans, and their animals. It was Ludwig Wittgenstein (1889–1951), a modern philosopher, who gave us the pithy, but profound observation, that: "The limits of my language mean the limits of my world."[16]

---

16. Wittgenstein, *Tractus Logico-Philosophicus*, 68.

It stands to reason, then, that to develop a culture we need to develop its language, including its symbols, customs, festivals, etc. Today, we have moved much more to visual forms of communication, which is where we need to apply our efforts at refinement and development. We need to work on a visual language that crosses the many cultural boundaries around us. Mere words, as Wittgenstein reminds us, can cause much misunderstanding. They are conditioned by the paradigms of daily life, by the forms and tones of human relationships.

Cardinal Lercaro, during the Council's debates on the *Pastoral Constitution*, called for a new language:

> The Church's culture must be given a new direction, especially in the institutions devoted to the formation of its students and to learned research... What hope can there be of lasting and promising dialogue if those who speak in the name of the church, priests and faithful, are educated in a program of studies which is completely out of date? If the learned language in which they have to think, for all its merits, is now dead, if it is no longer universal and is incapable of expressing the new ideas which are current everywhere in the world?[17]

In the Church, we have a long way to go to implement Cardinal Lercaro's words. We need to review the words in our common worship, catechisms, and diocesan newspapers. Do they still touch the hearts and minds of the people today? Are these ancient words still Good News? Are they gender inclusive? Do they express the inner faith of today's believers? Do they sparkle with visual imagery?

CONTEMPLATION

Article 59 of the *Pastoral Constitution* is also concerned with the cultivation of the human spirit. It tells us that the "*human spirit must be cultivated* in such a way that there results a growth in its ability *to wonder, to understand, to contemplate*, to make personal judgments, and to develop a religious, moral, and social sense."[18] These words have greater urgency today than ever before. Our busy hi-tech way of life does not foster, or even allow room for, contemplation.

---

17. CDVII 283.
18. DVII, No. 265. [Italics mine].

To combat the ever-increasing encroachment of distraction, we need to schedule some retreat time into our busy days—a half hour, or even an hour, sitting under our favorite tree in the backyard, where there are no TVs, radios, or cell phones. In these quiet places, we need to read and pray over any of the letters of St. Paul. Or, we need to go to the riverbank for an afternoon of contemplation, with the word of God, and the clouds, birds, water, and stray dogs as our only companions. We simply have to nourish and "cultivate" the contemplative side of our life; otherwise, we run the risk becoming deformed. After all, "a cultivated human spirit" is essential to a normal human existence.

Contemplation is also a condition for effective goal-setting. There is no sense in 'making good time' in our car in the middle of the night if we don't know where we are going. A well developed culture knows where it is going. But much depends on the contemplative abilities of the individual members of a culture or society. Otherwise, the culture itself will run over the cliff; or, into a bloody war.

Certainly there are more ways to develop our many cultures, but we have to start somewhere. And, hopefully, the suggestions given above at least have the potential to stimulate prayerful discernment and imaginative creativity.

QUESTIONS FOR DISCUSSION

1. Why is dialogue called "A Sacred Art?"
2. In what ways do you hold yourself accountable to your parish or diocesan community?
3. In the interpretation of language across cultures what are some of the biggest obstacles?
4. Are there any words, phrases, symbols in the Sunday Liturgy that are just "Greek" to you? Can you name them?
5. Do you have a favorite place for daily contemplation? A favorite time?
6. What do the "Arts" have to do with proper development? What is your favorite? Why?

7

Our Faith and Inculturation

SOME DEFINITIONS

First, we need some definitions of our new terms. Recall that we defined 'culture' at some length in Chapter I. We discovered that culture is a human product, and we learned that we shape our culture or our culture shapes us. Now, we meet a somewhat trickier word, 'inculturation.' Here we are actually concerned with two fairly new words, viz. 'inculturation' and 'enculturation.' They sound the same, but each actually means something a little different. "Inculturation," as Fr. Pedro Arrup SJ defines it, is:

> The incarnation of Christian life and of the Christian message in a particular cultural context in such a way that this experience not only finds expression through elements proper to the culture in question (this alone would be no more than a superficial adaptation) but becomes a principle that animates, directs, and unifies the culture, transforming it and remaking it so as to bring about a 'new creation'[1]

Perhaps the most important part of this definition is contained in the last phrase: "becomes a principle that animates, directs and unifies the culture, transforming it and remaking it so as to bring about a 'new creation.'" The words "transforming and remaking" fit rather well with the idea of development as explained by the *Pastoral Constitution*. They also remind us of Jesus' parable: "The kingdom of heaven is like a leaven which a woman took and hid in three measures of meal..." (Mt. 13:33). "Leaven" is a change agent. So our faith, since it is a way of life, will have to change the culture in which we live. So we, as believers, are a dynamic force in our culture moving it toward a "new creation."

---

1. Quoted in Aylward Shorter, *Toward a Theology of Inculturation*, 11.

"Enculturation," on the other hand, has a more sociological connotation. It "refers to the cultural learning process of the individual, the process by which a person is inserted into his or her culture."[2] Enculturation refers to the individual in culture; inculturation refers to the culture itself. While the two words are linked in many ways, they highlight two different aspects of a dynamic process. "Enculturation" is a sociological process whereby the individual appropriates the meaning of the culture's signs and symbols into his/her life. Thus, it has a strongly subjective element. We cannot live in a culture without being influenced or even transformed by it. But individuals appropriate the culture's signs and symbols in their own unique way. The individual's act of receiving the culture's message reshapes it in the image of the receiver.

FAITH-FILLED CULTURES

Now we need to ask how our faith transforms or develops our culture? By faith we do not mean merely believing a list of abstract truths such as the Nicene Creed. Faith is not something we have, but is something we are. Faith is a way of being. Thus, a believer feeding the hungry within any culture becomes part of the process of transforming and remaking his\her culture. The same is true of those who cloth the naked, visit the sick, and give drink to the thirsty, or make peace in time of war, etc. Ultimately, these are actions of believers transforming their culture by living out their Christian values. Again, these values are not a list of truths, but are the incarnation of Jesus in the flesh and the Risen Christ with all his transforming power. Thus faith, like Jesus of Nazareth, always exists in some kind of living embodiment within a specific culture. And, since the Incarnation and Resurrection, our culture is always in a process of transformation. Interculturalism, on account of this, will be contagious. A faith-filled culture, by its very nature, will be a transforming culture. It will infuse its neighboring cultures with Christian values and, through the power of the Risen Christ, will transform them into a new creation.

Throughout this process the faith-filled culture will be a living reflection both of the historical Jesus in the flesh and the risen Lord now transformed. Critical to the success of this process is for the faith-filled culture to re-live and reflect both the earthly sweat and blood of Jesus and the glorious risen Christ. But, for the process to work the faith-filled

2. Ibid., 5.

culture has to keep the two together. For this reason a brief review of the earthly Jesus may help.

The historical Jesus was a Jewish peasant. His given name was Yeshua, a name quite common among the Hebrew men of that time; it is actually an Aramaic form of Joshua, the hero who led the Jewish people into the Promised Land. Jesus (a later Greek form of Yeshua) was called Yeshua *of Nazareth* to distinguish Him from all the other men called Yeshua; this also followed the ancient custom whereby a person was known and identified by his or her tie to a location or a region. As a devout Jewish male, Jesus observed all the Jewish laws and customs, including the rite of circumcision and the dietary laws. He also spoke Aramaic, the Semitic language of the culture at that time, and attended the synagogue services, worshiping with his Jewish family and community. He was often called 'Rabbi,' in recognition of his knowledge and abilities as a teacher. Jesus was a living part—a member—of the history, the daily toils and concerns, of the Jewish culture of the first century. In other words, God, in the act of incarnation—in taking on human flesh in Jesus—became incarnate in a specific time and culture. Jesus Christ, in his fully human existence, was not just a generic human being; he was a particular Jewish human person. The cultural condition of the incarnation—and its political magnitude—is reflected in the placard hung above the cross upon which he died, which declared him to be 'King of the Jews.'

Among all the diverse cultures on earth in Jesus' time, God chose to become "incultured" in the Jewish culture with all its particularities, virtues, and even faults. So, divine revelation comes to us through the historical words, signs, feasts, and symbols of a specific culture. Occupied by the powerful Roman Empire, the Jewish culture of Jesus' time was mixed—a multicultural society. Palestinian society was flush with Rome's tax collectors, politicians, such as Pontius Pilate, who was the Roman procurator, and, more visibly, the Roman soldiers. So, the Jewish culture during the era of Jesus' lifetime was fully interpenetrated by a foreign culture, with the consequent tensions and cultural clashes. The power of Caesar was never absent, continually seen and felt by all. The official language of the Roman Empire, at that time, was Greek, as a result of the cultural cohesion that occurred a few centuries prior (i.e., the extended campaigns of Alexander the Great); the New Testament itself was written in Greek, indicating the common (or universal) vision at its base. So, in the first century context of a Jewish culture intersected by Roman and Greek cultural identities, divine revelation comes to us through a three-fold *intercultural* matrix.

From a theological perspective, the basis for our understanding of culture, and the processes involved in cultural intersection, is the mystery of the Incarnation. The Incarnation of Jesus Christ—as fully God and fully human—provides a distinct vantage point from which to understand the dynamic involved. On the one hand, the Incarnation is an act of God—becoming a concrete, particular human being—which is located at specific point in space and time, including the common features of a particular culture. Even more, the crucifixion, the crucial saving act of Christ, was an event isolable to a time and place. On the other hand, in the resurrection, the event of the Incarnation is opened up in a transcendent way such that not only does the Incarnation continue, but is now unlimited by the contingencies of time or space. The saving action of Christ continues in and through all cultures where, and in whatever forms, they exist. Thus, saving grace, in the Incarnation and through the resurrection, is not restricted by any factor; even the sacraments, while administered in particular place and at specific times, do not limit grace within the confines of institutions, time, or space. Grace just is unlimited and everywhere, whether explicitly or implicitly.

Like the former marks of the church, our faith-filled culture has some distinctive marks. First, it is distinguished by its Christian hospitality. This culture remembers the blessed words of Paul to the Romans: "Practice hospitality" (Rom 12:13). Secondly, this faith-filled culture is marked by its compassion, forgiveness, and reconciliation. This compassion has no limits because the compassion of Jesus has no limits. Thirdly, this culture is deeply sensitive to the needs of the common good. Thus, it understands quickly, for instance, that the pollution of God's created world is a moral issue. Faith-filled culture responds daily to social justice issues, like the rights of the poor and the victims of racism. Fourthly, it will be distinguished also by Christian joy and optimism. This will be a Christian optimism because it is based on the power of the Resurrection to overcome evil in whatever form it exists. Under the impulse of the power of the Resurrection, this culture exorcizes evil though the power of the Risen Christ. Thus, a faith-filled culture will be an example to the many cultures that surround us today. Linked to the Light of Christ, it will become a light leading the Christian pilgrimage to the promised land.

Our Faith and Inculturation

In view of all the above, and in view of our pluralistic culture, we have to be more concerned with *inter*culturation than with *en*culturation, although both are part of an ongoing process. Our global mobility, and the influx of Asian, African, and Latino/a cultures add to the earlier Irish, Italian, French, Polish, and German cultures of previous generations of immigration. This means that, in the U.S., we have a grand mixture—a garden salad—of cultures, intermingling in all areas of our society. In this context, the question is raised concerning into which of these many cultures will the new cultures 'enculturate.' We have to admit that, in the current political rhetoric coming out of Western culture, the word *enculturation* is not free from a certain imperialist and condescending connotation. It assumes that the new incoming cultures must assimilate into a distinct, identifiable culture not their own. There is no doubt that our U.S. culture is still predominantly Western, but, beyond that, our distinctiveness quickly fades into undefined, vague pluralism. The best we can do now is interact, interrelate, and *inter*culturate. Since these new incoming cultures maintain their distinct cultures, the old image of the 'melting pot' is daily becoming less descriptive of the current reality of culture in the U.S. As Christians, we must embrace the new cultures as they are; they cannot be required to 'melt' into some other culture before they are welcome at their common table.

On the other hand, unless our new cultures resist assimilation completely, and settle in some kind of isolated desert enclave, some 'melting' will necessarily take place. All cultures obey the same laws and are heavily influenced by the same media. But, we cannot enforce such melting, imposing our own standards upon others; any kind of assimilation must come naturally and at the will of our new neighbors. The vision we have in mind is stated most aptly in a page from the Chinese Hundred Flowers Campaign (1956–57): "Let a hundred flowers bloom together, let the hundred schools of thought contend."[3] Although that philosophy did not work in the context of China, it may work in our present situation.

Our various cultures are enriched daily by interacting and intermingling with each other. The Church, since it is partly a human institution, is also enriched by the processes of interacting and interculturating. Moreover, the Church, as a living body, is always enculturating and interculturating at the same time, and has recognized and accepted this truth

---

3. Fairbank and Goldman, *China*, 364.

in varying degrees throughout most of its history. We turn, now, to a few examples of these processes.

ENCULTURATION

Enculturation is manifest from the beginning in the Hebrew scriptures. For example, it is quite evident in Genesis one, which leans heavily on the surrounding Mesopotamian culture, where we find many stories of the beginnings of the world. Scripture scholars have noted the similarities between the accounts of creation contained in Genesis, the epic poem of Gilgamesh called the Enuma Elish, and the Atrahasis story. Close comparison reveals that the Genesis stories of creation were written as a polemic against the Mesopotamian and Canaanite myths of creation.[4] But, even as a 'counter-narrative' to these other stories, the Genesis account employs the same forms and images as these early myths, perhaps even borrowing directly from them.

The Psalms, which make up a good part of the Divine Office, as the official prayer book of the Church, "generally borrow themes, style and rhythm from the Canaanite hymns. Psalm 29 is a striking example."[5] Additionally, the Book of Wisdom is a Jewish work, but "its literary form and structure ... are entirely Greek ... There are allusions to Hellenistic culture, thought, and values ...The book is ... a successful example of inculturation."[6] The Septuagint, the Greek translation of the Hebrew Bible made in Alexandria about 250 BCE, is actually an interpretation of the Hebrew scriptures influenced by Greek ideas. In the text of the Septuagint, Hebrew words, such as the name of God (*Yahweh*), are replaced by Greek words like *Kyrios* (Lord), which have deep roots in the Hellenistic culture. Thus, in this version of the Hebrew Bible, the Word of God *incorporates* the surrounding culture into the fabric of the text.

We have already noted that the New Testament is heavily influenced, not only by Judaism, but also by the Graeco-Roman culture. When the historical Jesus took a prophetic stand against particular elements within the Jewish culture of his time, the Jewish framework for His message is no-

---

4. See the *New Jerome Biblical Commentary*, s.v. "Genesis," 8; see also the footnote to Psalm 29: "Several expressions in this psalm are also found in the Canaanite texts written in the fifteenth century B.C. at Ugarit."

5. Shorter, *Toward a Theology of Enculturation*, 109.

6. Ibid., 115–16.

tably visible. At other moments, the language or symbols appropriated by Jesus in delivering his message to people comes directly from the Roman presence in that environment—of which the people of that time would have been highly aware. The proper interpretation of Jesus' message, then, must attend closely to the context of the laws, symbols, and customs of the Jewish and Graeco-Roman cultures. God's Word, proclaimed through the historical Jesus, is not a disembodied Word, but is enfleshed and clothed in the bodies of the surrounding cultures. That is one form of inculturation. We cannot get to the meaning of the Word of God without first going through, or appreciating, the historical culture that shaped the text. And, that culture is part of the meaning that needs to be translated in our own culture before it becomes enfleshed in our own lives.

As noted in the last chapter, St. Augustine (354–430), reading deeply in Plotinus, an ancient philosopher who reinterpreted Plato, leaned heavily on the Greek culture of the Platonists. According to David Knowles, Augustine "accepted the teaching of the Platonists as successful attempts to reach the truth about the universe so far as man's mind could go."[7] Augustine believed that, since all of nature was created by the one God, both nature and reason could reveal truth about God. Supernatural revelation, through Jesus Christ, was one source of truth; nature, including human reason, and even the Greek culture, was another.

St. Thomas Aquinas (1225–74), also noted in the last chapter, accepted most of the rational Greek philosophy of Aristotle. Aquinas incorporated much of Aristotle's teaching in his famous *Summa Theologica*, which became the guiding light for scholastic theology. This theology, in turn, had a profound influence upon the Council of Trent (1545–1563), which articulated the true faith against the deviations of the Protestants. It is clear that the Church, rather than forming its own independent Catholic culture, brought other cultures into its own system. The Church's ecclesiology, in its external historical forms, has been a fluid process of synthesizing through most of its history.

We cannot forget that the Latin Rite Code of Canon Law appropriated many of the civil laws of the Roman Empire. Gratian, a professor at the University of Bologna, commissioned by Pope Gregory VII, published his famous *Harmony of Discordant Canons* in 1141. He selectively eliminated laws that contradicted each other, while giving priority to the

---

7. Knowles, "Introduction," in *Augustine: City of God*, xxiv.

Roman legal system. Gratian also ignored the Chinese legal code, which was well advanced for that time.[8] Pope Gregory VII earlier had eliminated the Frankish and Celtic legal systems as bases for Canon law. Thus, the Roman legal collection became the source for most of the collections of ecclesiastical law, including the famous Code of Canon Law published in 1917. Thus, much of the legal system of the Roman culture was incorporated into the official laws of the Catholic Church. But, it was assumed, in view of the Incarnation, that God was not absent in the formulation of laws by other cultures. The Roman legal system, perhaps through the grace of God, was also quite advanced for that time. However, we cannot dismiss the possibility that Roman imperialism may have played some role in the adoption of the Roman legal system. From the standpoint of the humanity of the Church, it will always be vulnerable to secular influence. Specific forms of inculturation, though, can go too far. The universal Church, in a certain sense, has to transcend all earthly cultures, so that it may not become overly inculturated within one culture; otherwise, its inculturation may become an obstacle to its mission to the other cultures of the world. Inculturation is a process that goes on with detachment and continuing discernment. Inculturation is an historical process. Thus it cannot become an absolute, as if it were a defined dogma. The results of the transforming process are limited by a specific time in history. These can be changed by future movements of the Spirit, who blows where and when He wills.

The global mission of the Church does not mean the homogenization of form; rather, it involves translating its universal message *into* forms that are understandable to, and at home in, other cultures. Thus, we witness, for example, that during the African Synod of bishops in 1994, Africans publicly called for an African Council with power to legislate for that continent. The African bishops felt that they needed a non-Western, specifically African Code of Law that reflected the African culture. The indigenous (*autochthonous*) churches of Mexico share a similar concern with their African counterparts. The Church in Mexico also hopes that Rome will respect the "*Teologia India*, which finds its roots in lived experiences, in critical reflection, and in the transforming dynamics of the autochthonous churches."[9] There will always be some tensions between the local "enculturated" churches and the universal Catholic Church,

---

8. Fairbank and Goldman, *China*, 183.

9. María Pilar Aquino, "Theology and the Indigenous Cultures of the Americas: Conditions of Dialogue," *CTSA Proceedings*, 61/5, (June 2006), Appendix II.

though such tensions may be a healthy sign that the Body of Christ is a live, growing body.

In the Church, the various parts are really linked to the whole body. Inculturation of the universal Church, as it occurs in the movement and settlement of the Church into other cultures, needs to take place with a kind of detachment from its own internal culture. As the Church exists in a global setting, it must give up continuously that part of its own exportation into other cultures, which, through time, has become an obstacle to an effective mission to today's cultures. This remains especially true of the 'Roman' form of the Church's structures, as noted above. We must call to mind that Jesus never imposed inculturation into the Roman culture as a condition for salvation. On the other hand, if the Church is to remain a Catholic Church, all local churches need to respect their bonds of unity with the universal Church as a whole; that is, at the root, there is something shared, held in common, which fosters a deep, unbreakable connection across all locations. While a common law may not be the most important bond, it does enrich the local church with 2000 years of experience in the wider world. So, a universal code cannot be dismissed without some loss to the local church. Without such a code of common law, there is also the danger of the local church falling into a sect or into nationally oriented schism.

These examples demonstrate that the tradition of inculturation and interculturation of the faith is well established in the Catholic Church. After the Resurrection, the Church cannot be bound to a particular time of history or to a particular culture. It embraces all cultures with equal respect for God's presence in its manifold forms. Although the ministry of the historical Jesus was confined to the Jewish culture, the risen Lord is no longer bound to any one culture. In approaching a new culture, the Church comes with awe, respect, and, even, reverence. For, saving grace has never been bound to human clocks, calendars, or earthly human boundaries.

INCULTURATION

Though the instances we have examined so far seem to indicate that inculturation is a one-way street, this is not so. Inculturation of the faith is always a two-way process. It is best defined as "the ongoing dialogue between faith and culture or cultures. More fully, it is the creative and dynamic relationship between the Christian message and a culture or cultures."[10] We have already reviewed, in an earlier chapter, the failure that occurred in the Church's attempt at inculturation into the Chinese culture. But, we can also learn more from the relative successes of inculturation that have occurred in Africa, especially in Zaire, Cameroon, and Zimbabwe.

These successes can be attributed, at least in part, to the Church's respect and reverence for the African culture as it is, even though it may seem strange, or exotic, upon first contact. The Zaire Mass and the Zimbabwe funeral rite serve as successful forms of Catholic inculturation in these regions. An enculturated church will always need to express itself in different forms of worship, becoming a unity expressed in multiformity. Since cultures are always changing, the Church's forms of worship will have to change too. In terms of inculturation, we can be grateful that *The Pastoral Constitution* (No. 58) linked the Church with the changing cultures which receive the faith, and, in turn, re-express that faith through their own unique cultures. Under the inspiration of the Holy Spirit, inculturation is always an ongoing process, in which the Word is always becoming flesh in a new way. Inculturation is the Word's outward expression and incarnation in a specific time and culture. That is how the Word continues to become a saving Word to a specific culture and people, by establishing itself fully within their midst.

Through most of its history the Church has supported diverse rites of worship that incorporate distinct elements of native cultures. Thus Popes, Cardinals, and bishops have supported, for instance, the Greek-Melkite rite. Cardinal Lavigerie, Archbishop of Algiers, had some strong words for the school administrators of the Apostolic School of St. Anne, which was established for Eastern rite Catholics: "The children must never be made to adopt the Latin rite."[11] Since the close of Vatican II, at least six different Eucharistic prayers have been approved: Germany, the Philippines, Switzerland, Australia, the Netherlands, and Brazil each have their own Eucharistic prayers. The Liturgy of a particular country is the outward expression of the Church and its unique culture. We have noted earlier that the Church has nine different rites—*all of local origin*. Most of the Eastern rites, in fact, are older than the Latin rite.

---

10. Shorter, *Toward a Theology of Inculturation*, 1.
11. For more details see Shorter, 170.

Our Faith and Inculturation

The blessings of inculturation are aptly described by the *Pastoral Constitution*:

> The Good News of Christ continually renews the life and culture of fallen man; it combats and removes the error and evil which flow from the ever-present attraction of sin. It never ceases to purify and elevate the morality of peoples. It takes the spiritual qualities and endowments of every age and nation, and with supernatural riches it causes them to blossom, as it were, from within; it fortifies, completes and restores them in Christ. In this way the Church carries out its mission and in that very act it stimulates and advances human and civil culture, as well contributing by its activity, including liturgical activity, to man's interior freedom.[12]

These powerful words of the Council leave no doubt about the good that can come to human society through inculturation. They also motivate us to bend our energies to accomplish the goals of inculturation. In doing so, we constantly need to be sensitive to the three-way dynamics. Peter Phan articulates these dynamics, arguing that inculturation "is always *interculturation*. It is an encounter among at least three different cultures—of the Bible, of the Christian tradition, and of the people to whom the Gospel is proclaimed."[13]

Just as the Jewish culture became the vehicle of saving grace in and through Christ Jesus, so the various cultures of today can become instruments of the saving grace of the risen Christ. Cultures, like the waters of baptism, can become sacraments of salvation for those who seek the waters of life. The baptismal waters may be dirty—humanly imperfect—and a mixture of good and evil, but that does not nullify the awesome power of saving grace present in culture.

THE ROLE OF LANGUAGE IN INCULTURATION

Pope John XXIII, in his opening address to the Council, alerted the Church to the importance of language in the whole process of inculturation. His statement was brief, but extremely significant: "For the substance of the ancient doctrine of the faith is one thing, and the way in which it

---

12. *Vatican Council II*, ed. Austin Flannery, O.P., No. 58. (I have used the Flannery Edition because I feel it has the better translation).
13. Phan, *Being Religious Interreligiously*, 242.

is presented is another."[14] All of our teaching, including the truths of our faith, is expressed in historical symbols and languages, which are fluid and constantly vary with the changing cultures. Based upon this, it is evident that inculturation will require considerable sensitivity to the language and features of each culture, including its festivals, symbols, and many unspoken forms of communication. Sometimes the cultural context of a word or symbol is more important than the word itself; so, for example, a painting of Our Lady of Guadalupe in Mexico reveals the nature and shape of the devotional practices of a specific Latino/a culture.

Older readers may be familiar with the term adaptation, especially as applied to missionary activity in foreign lands. However, the bishops of Africa, in their demand for an African Council and the development of an African legal canon and rites, rightly wanted to go beyond mere adaptation. While upholding firmly the true Catholic faith, they are moving toward a pluralism of theological and liturgical form. There is no doubt that since Vatican II, and especially since the *Pastoral Constitution*, theological pluralism is a significant component of inculturation. Without such a vision, theology loses its pastoral dimension by being a vertical imposition of already determined formulations that do not necessarily fit the local—horizontal—spaces. Theology, as noted earlier, develops both from above and from below; and, insofar as it develops "from below," it will become pastoral and pluralist through attention to and appreciation of the particular context and location.

The Holy Spirit enlivens theology through "the sense of faith which is aroused and sustained by the Spirit of Truth"[15] from below, within the People of God. Thus, both dimensions are necessary for a complete theology, which has the Incarnation of the Word as its cornerstone. For this reason, mere adaptation is not enough. Theology, like the Word itself, has to express itself through the various cultures, otherwise it will no longer speak the Word of life. Unless that Word becomes incarnate in the new culture, it will not be a saving, life-giving Word to that culture; rather, it will become nothing more than an inward-turning, academic exercise.

Bishop Donald Trautman, of Erie, PA, has waged a long and difficult campaign for better translations of our English Liturgy. In a recent article, he asks the pertinent question: "Is [our] prayer intelligible, proclaimable,

---

14. Abbott, S. J. "Pope John's Opening Speech," 715.
15. Abbott S. J., ed., *The Dogmatic Constitution on the Church*, in DVII, 29.

and reflective of a vocabulary and linguistic style from the contemporary mainstream of U.S. Catholics? Is the liturgical language accessible to the average Catholic and our youth?" Further, he explains that liturgical texts "must be owned by the people and expressed in the contemporary language of their culture . . . If the liturgical language is divorced from the reality of culture, communication is impossible."[16] The same holds true for our homilies, our pastoral letters, and our theological language; otherwise, our words are no longer saving, life-giving words.

All of the above indicates the importance of indigenous leaders who speak and live the language of the various cultures. Missionaries, including lay ecclesial ministers, need to work themselves out of a job by tutoring indigenous replacements. When we die, the programs we lead should not die with us. If they do, we have not been serving Christ or our churches. Training new indigenous leaders is an important part of inculturation.

THE "HOW TO" OF INCULTURATION

In our individualistic culture, inculturation will be difficult. Cross-cultural interaction will bring with it many tensions, arguments, and, at first, some misunderstandings which seem irreconcilable. But, by the grace of God, it will also bring about the surprising mutual enrichment of diversity and, eventually, peace, harmony, and a loving community, at the local and national levels respectively. Inculturation will bring its own unforeseen rewards. Humans, with their inherent dignity, and from whatever culture, gathering in prayer and dialogue, will experience a brother/sisterhood that is a preview of heavenly joy.

To move toward inculturation, we need to initiate a process of interaction, interrelating, and intermingling. The first step toward inculturation, therefore, as noted above, is *inter*culturation. Interculturation will require real dialogue, as we previously defined in the last chapter. Listening with full attention of heart and mind will be the hardest, but most vital, part. Dialogue is the key that opens doors and hearts to the new world of the other, 'strange' cultures.

In order for this to be effective, dialogue must be structured; otherwise, in our individualistic culture, real exchange will never happen, and we will keep going on our busy way, barely acknowledging one another,

---

16. Trautman, "How Accessible Are the New Mass Translations?" *America* 18 (May 21, 2007): 10–11.

turning us into passing cultures. To make it work requires determination and deliberation, such as scheduling a meeting, however informal, over coffee and donuts, or something similar. And then, at the end of coffee, we need to initiate the question of whether such an encounter can happen again—here we make in-roads. We will soon find occasion to volunteer our talents to help someone from a culture other than our own. In so doing, we build the reciprocity that is the life of the dialogue. Importantly, when we generate commonality and mutuality, differences become accepted with humor and respect. In time, we will discover that what cultures have in common exceeds their differences. From the vantage point of understanding and appreciating both the shared points of contact and the differences that exists amongst cultures, we are on our way to true interculturation. This will pave the way for the first level of inculturation—social friendships.

INTERFAITH INTERCULTURAL COMMUNITIES

The next step toward interculturation will be the formation of small interfaith communities. These small communities will follow the models of the base communities of Latin America, and the small Christian communities of the highly successful Renew Programs. Theologically, they will also be modeled on the Vatican II documents, *Decree on Ecumenism* and *Nostra Aetate, the Declaration on the Relationship of the Church to Non-Christian Religions*. Fundamentally, according to these conciliar statements, Catholics, Protestants, Muslims, Jews, Buddhists, atheists, etc., of whatever culture, will belong to these communities. "In ecumenical work," states the *Decree on Ecumenism*, "Catholics must assuredly be concerned for their separated brethren, praying for them, keeping them informed about the church, *making the first approaches toward them*."[17]

Underlining the notion of an interfaith ecumenism, in *Nostra Aetate*, Vatican II speaks favorably of many of the world's religions, including Islam, Hinduism, Buddhism, Judaism, and Christianity. The text urges us "to forget the centuries of quarrels and hostilities," eliciting calls for "respect" and "brotherly dialogues;" the open attitude of the Council is encapsulated in a further, rather powerful, passage:

> The Catholic Church rejects nothing which is true and holy in these religions. She looks with sincere respect upon those ways of conduct and of life, those rules and teachings which, though differing

17. DVII, No. 4. [Italics mine].

Our Faith and Inculturation

in many particulars from what she holds and sets forth, nevertheless often reflect a ray of that Truth which enlightens all men.[18]

These two Vatican II decrees provide the theological foundation for the formation of small interfaith communities. Such communities will be intercultural from the beginning, and all cultures will be equal within these communities—there is no religious cultural hierarchy. Thus the discussions will be aimed not at conversion, but rather at interaction, interrelating, and deeper mutual understanding through shared prayer, study and reflection.

Daniel S. Mulhall has six excellent practical suggestions for building these kinds of inclusive communities in the parish:

1. Know your people
2. Set up a multicultural advisory committee.
3. Work for the complementarity of cultures.
4. Develop structures to deal with cultural tensions
5. Encourage conversation and interaction.
6. Listen.[19]

Of the six suggestions, no doubt, "listen," as opposed to talk, or even hear, as discussed in the previous chapter, deserves the top priority. Of course, some one has to talk if there is going to be conversation and interaction; but, given the hyperactivity of our culture, the art of real listening, with heart and soul, has become a rare ability today, and needs to be the subject of intentional cultivation. Moments of silence can become holy times of meditation, a time to process before engaging in speech.

Regarding the format of such communities, there are available options. Some communities will be seasonal; others will meet year round. They should have eight to twelve members with a trained facilitator, as they need to be small enough to develop real intimacy, but overseen by someone who can trigger engagement and guide participants together in discovery. Together, through consensus, the community itself will determine the topics to be discussed. They will decide on the internal structure—of days and times of meetings, and the schedule for each meeting. In organizing such communities, it will be necessary to assemble a core team

---

18. Ibid., No. 2.
19. Mulhall, "Building Inclusive Communities," *America* 196 (5 February 2007): 21–22.

to train facilitators, recruit members, provide study and resource materials, and build communities across the cultural boundaries. This team will clarify the goals, objectives, and strategies for the meetings. Thus, the core team will need time, personnel, and relational and teaching skills. Most of the time the actual communities will be built through mutual support, phone calls, e-mails, and sharing daily concerns. This will be a challenging task across different cultures. But, relating interculturally at the deeper levels of faith, values, and customs will bring its own reward

Whatever our culture, we are social animals capable of refining and developing our human condition. But, some one with initiative, creativity, organizing talent, and considerable patience has to organize the whole process. Over time, interculturation will become our own reality, even within our individualistic, yet pluralist, culture. Once we have achieved true interculturation, we will be well on our way to inculturation of the various cultures. All of the above assumes that all participants speak some kind of common language, or are at least willing to learn it. There is no reason why one community could not speak Spanish and the other, English. As time goes on, language will become less and less of a barrier.

A good supply of "how to" resource materials is available at the National Pastoral Life Center, 18 Bleecker St., New York, NY 10012-2404.[20]

QUESTIONS FOR DISCUSSION

1. What is the difference between interculturation and inculturation? Which comes first? Why?
2. What challenges do you foresee in starting an Interfaith Intercultural Community?
3. How many of the various rites in the church can you name? How do they relate to culture?
4. What can the African inculturation bring to the rest of the world's cultures?
5. How can we be "the leaven" and "the salt of the earth" in the public domain? Like on our school board? Our city council?
6. Do you feel you are an active partner in a faith-filled culture?

---

20. Perhaps the best booklet on the inner dynamics of these kinds of small communities is authored by Arthur Baranowski, *Pastoring the Pastors* (Cincinnati, OH: St. Anthony Messenger Press, 1988).

8

An Unsung Prophet

In truth I can affirm that were I to recount the vile acts committed here, the exterminations, the massacres, the cruelties, the violence and sinfulness against God and the King of Spain, I would write a very big book.[1]

—Bartolomé de las Casas

IF THERE IS A patron saint for the ministers of interculturation, it is most certainly Bartolomé de las Casas (1484–1566). He was a scholar, historian, the first Bishop of Chiapas (now in Mexico), and an energetic advocate of the rights of native peoples. With all the power at his command, he opposed the racism and imperialism of his native Spain. Las Casas fought for the repeal of Spanish laws that reduced the native 'Indians' of Latin America to slaves and serfs. In forceful spoken and written words, befitting a true prophet, Las Casas opposed the slaughter, torture, cruelty, and enslavement of the Amerindians. While it is the case that his efforts were directed towards a single culture, his example may point the way forward for the interculturation of other cultures.

A HISTORICAL PERSPECTIVE

Born in Seville, Spain, in 1484, Bartolomé de las Casas was steeped in the Spanish culture of his day. Although we know nothing about his mother, we know his father was a merchant with a business of his own. While helping his father with his business, Las Casas also studied Latin and the required subjects of his time. At eighteen he completed his studies, but did not formally receive his degree because he could not afford the traditional fee presented to the faculty.

1. *The Devastation of the Indies*, trans. Herman Briffault, 89.

THE SPANISH CULTURE (C. 1500)

To set the context for our discussion, we will take up a brief description of the Spanish culture which shaped and conditioned Las Casas during his early years. Spain, like other European countries at that time, was ruled by a monarchy. Las Casas had to deal with the Emperor, Charles V (1500–1558), during most of his missionary activity in the New World. The imperial policy of Charles V was oriented toward the expansion of Spanish control into other lands, both to acquire material enrichment and to proclaim the Gospel so as to convert the natives to Christianity (and hence into proper Spanish subjects—into the Church, under the crown). It was widely believed at that time that those outside the Church—the unbaptized—were destined for damnation; for the Spanish monarchy, conversion of the natives opened the possibilities of providing a religious good (baptism) to natives, and expropriating native goods to itself (natural resources). It is clear, though, that for the Spanish conquistadores involved in these 'missions,' finding gold was a greater motivator than spreading the Gospel.

At this time, the union of Church and State was very tight in Spain. The Emperor appointed all the bishops, and had a large, controlling voice in Church government. According to Paul Johnson, Charles V "was in effect the head of the Church ... The order of royal coronations was strikingly similar to that used for the consecration of a bishop ... Both king and bishop were invested with ring and staff ... vestments worn were almost exactly the same ... The emperor was like a bishop only he had many more duties."[2]

The Church, at that time, taught that the union of Church and State was the ideal system of government for all countries. The fact that Pope Urban II could go to Clermont, France, in 1095, and, in a rousing speech, rally the French to take up arms in the Crusades against the Muslims is just one indication of the close union of Church and State that existed. Since the reign of Constantine (313), normative shape of the relationship between the Church and government was an indissoluble union between the ecclesial structure and political leadership, particularly monarchs and emperors. During the medieval era in Europe, it was not unusual for the political head of a nation or territory to exercise control over the affairs and the structure of the Church within the area of his or her domain; for

---

2. Johnson, *A History of Christianity*, 193.

example, in 1500, Spain "controlled its own Church, both at home and over seas . . . The Inquisition," authorized and supervised by the political powers, "was a popular instrument, directed mainly against Jews and Moors."[3] The rule of King Ferdinand and Queen Isabella gives us some further insight into this aspect of Spanish culture:

> Ferdinand and Isabella asserted their authority in religious as well as political matters. They carried out a full-scale reformation of the Church within their realms to root out corruption and to bring the Church more firmly under the authority of the crown. Their attempts at reform were remarkably successful.[4]

As recently as 1864, Pope Pius IX, in his famous "Syllabus of Errors," had condemned the separation of Church and State: "The Church ought to be separated from the State and the State from the Church" (Error no. 55). It was not until the Second Vatican Council (1962–65) that the Church officially declared "in their proper spheres, the political community and the Church are mutually independent and self-governing."[5] Las Casas, therefore, grew up in a culture in which a strong union of Church and State was taken for granted by everyone. And, it was a culture that, with the blessing of the Church, could apply force both in its own country and in its 'territories' whenever it felt it necessary. Spain, at that time, had one of the most powerful standing armies in the known Western world; and, on the sea, its fleet controlled the western Mediterranean. This was the world of Las Casas during his early years in Spain—a world in which the Church and imperial power were virtually wedded under the signet of the crown, and put into effect often in tandem.

SLAVERY

The long Christian tradition has supported slavery ever since St. Paul sent the slave, Onesimus, back to Philemon without any attempt to change the outward social structure of slavery (Phil. 12). Slavery, as an institution, gained considerable support when, during the scholastic period, Aristotle's teachings on social hierarchy gained entrance into Christian philosophy and theology. Aristotle taught that slavery, in fact, was part of the natural order: "He explains that the state is made up of households

---

3. Ibid., 297.
4. Cantor, *The Civilization of the Middle Ages*, 512.
5. DVII, No. 76.

'and the first and fewest parts of a family are master and slave, husband and wife, father and children.'"[6]

The institution of slavery received additional support from the ecclesial institution, whereby several popes in the medieval Church set out instructions for political rulers on the process of enslavement of native populations. Pope Nicholas V (1452–54) decreed:

> We grant you (Kings of Spain and Portugal) by these present documents, with our Apostolic Authority, full and free permission to invade, search out, capture, and subjugate the Saracens and pagans and any other unbelievers and enemies of Christ wherever they may be, as well as their kingdoms, duchies, counties, principalities, and other property ... and to reduce their persons into perpetual slavery."[7]

This Decree was confirmed by several popes in subsequent years; in 1493, Pope Alexander VI extended the provisions of the decree from Africa to America.[8]

Considering the strong union of Church and State in Spain, we are not surprised to discover that in the 'new world' the Spanish conquistadores, with this blessing of popes, would routinely enslave the native populations. This process was conducted through the dreaded *encomienda* system, which committed the natives into the care of a Spanish overlord. Las Casas reports that, under this system, a conquistador "would treat the whole of the native population—dignitaries, old men, women and children— as member of his household and, as such, make them labor night and day in his own interests, without any rest whatever; even the small children..."[9] All of this was an extension of the Spanish culture, part of the vision of the natural order.

IMPERIALISM

Las Casas came of age in an era of an ever-expanding European Empire, notably at the height of imperial Spanish power. He was, at least partly, conditioned by the Spanish culture's greed for power and wealth. Norman Cantor explains:

6. Boorstin, *The Seekers*, 55.
7. Fiedler and Rabben, *Rome has Spoken*, 82.
8. Ibid.
9. Griffen, *Bartolomé de las Casas*, 39.

An Unsung Prophet

When Christopher Columbus, flying the Spanish flag, landed in the islands off the coast of America on October 12, 1492, Spain possessed only the Canary Islands and the remnant of the Mediterranean empire of Aragon. Within a few decades it had the largest overseas empire among the European states. At the moment when the economy of the Mediterranean world was entering its last decades of prosperity, Spain was in the forefront of expansion of Europe into the unknown lands of America and the orient.[10]

The by-products of imperialism, whether Spanish or American, are arrogance, coercion, greed, torture, and profiteering.

U.S. political policy is also obsessed with empire-building, even though we do not call it that. The rhetoric about globalization is ultimately about extending the reach and power the U.S. throughout the world; this is particularly evident in the attempts to export democracy—to remake the world in our political image. It is invariably the case that those who are infected by the pathology of power, whether kings or presidents, always want more power. Expansion of power can take many forms, but it is always the result of an insatiable desire—no king or president ever gets up and says, 'Please do not give me any more power.' And "power," as the famous historian, Lord Acton (1834–1902), warned us, "tends to corrupt, and absolute power corrupts absolutely." Las Casas was not immune to the Spanish imperialist culture. So, when he spoke truth to power, as all prophets do, he had to transcend his own cultural conditioning of the Spanish imperialist greed for power.

THE SPANISH OCCUPATION

As noted in Chapter Three, Hernán Cortes, flying the Spanish flag, landed on the Island of Cozumel, Mexico, in 1519. For 300 years, until the signing of the treaty of Córdoba in 1821, Spain occupied the 'Indian' countries of this 'new world.' It was a cruel and painful period in the history of these innocent people. To begin to understand Bartolomé de las Casas' prophetic ministry, we need to see with his eyes what he witnessed in the behavior of his own countrymen. In 1541 the Spaniards arrived in large numbers in Hispaniola, which today includes Haiti and the Dominican Republic. What happened here was repeated in the other lands of the Americas. Las Casas reports just a few of the blood curdling details:

10. *The Civilization of the Middle Ages*, 513.

> They [the soldiers] forced their way into native settlements, slaughtering everyone they found there, including small children, old men, pregnant women, and even women who had just given birth. They hacked them to pieces, slicing open their bellies with their swords as though they were so many sheep herded into a pen. They even laid wagers on whether they could manage to slice a man in two at a stroke, or cut the individual's head from his body, or disembowel him with a single blow of their axes. They grabbed suckling infants by the feet, ripping them from their mothers' breasts, dashed them headlong against the rocks. Others, laughing and joking all the while threw them over their shoulders into a river, shouting: 'Wriggle, you little perisher.' They slaughtered anyone and everyone in their path, on occasion running through a mother and her baby with a single thrust of their swords. They spared no one, erecting especially wide gibbets on which they could string their victims up with their feet just off the ground and then burn them alive, thirteen at a time, in honor of our Savior and the twelve apostles, or tie dry straw to their bodies and set fire to it.[11]

With only minor variations, the conquistadores repeated these burnings, tortures, and massacres in Nicaragua, Mexico (New Spain), Panuco, Jalisco and the Yucatan in Mexico, Santa Marta, (Columbia), Trinidad Venezuela, and Peru. What did not vary was the dreaded *encomienda* system through which the Spanish forced the natives into slavery. The *encomienda* system, besides enjoying the blessing of the popes, had legal standing through legislation passed in Spain. On account of this, the conquistadores felt that they were fully within their legal rights to bind the conquered peoples into cruel slavery.

But the genocide perpetuated upon the innocent native inhabitants was even worse. Bartolomé de las Casas provides the heart-rending details of these occurrences in his *Short Account of the Destruction of the Indies*. Las Casas' accounts are first-hand reports, scenes he saw, as he reminds us repeatedly, with his very own eyes. For example, he recounts a cruel episode of the hanging of an elderly queen: "They strung her up and I saw with my own eyes how the Spaniards burned countless local inhabitants alive or hacked them to pieces, or devised novel ways of torturing them to death ... they invented so many new methods of murder that it would

---

11. Bartolomé de las Casas, *A Short Account of the Destruction of the Indies*, trans. Nigel Griffen, in *Bartolomé de las Casas*, 15.

An Unsung Prophet

be quite impossible to set them all down on paper . . .[12] What happened across the continent of the Americas was a holocaust before *the* Holocaust; a genocide before the term entered the parlance of the times.

The atrocities committed by the Germans against the Jewish people, and other people groups during World War II, rightly receives considerable publicity, even to this day. But, the genocide committed by the Spanish during their invasion of the Latino countries is still unknown to most Americans. This may be due to the continuing ignorance of the history of the many countries south of our own border. Except for the lonely voice of Bartolomé de las Casas, these poor peoples had no means to reach the eyes and ears of the rest of the world. Their pain and suffering went largely unnoticed. And this, unfortunately, remains true to this day.

The Hebrew Bible reminds us that the early history of the Jewish people was also one of bondage and enforced labor—the years of slavery in Egypt. After their escape, they rightly looked forward to an earthly paradise, a place with no overlords or slave masters, "a land flowing with milk and honey" (Deut 27:3). The German, Irish, and Italian immigrants, who came to the U.S. during the nineteenth century, were also looking for their own promised land. It is strange indeed that their descendants today are so slow to offer Christian hospitality to the Latino/a immigrants now coming into the U.S that their forefathers sought. They have suffered a long and cruel enslavement in their home countries, and are rightly looking forward to their own opportunities in the land of promise north of the U.S. border. The Latino/a migrants are looking for a new Bartolomé de las Casas, one who will lead them and speak for them.

BARTOLOMÉ DE LAS CASAS' PROPHETIC RESPONSE

We have noted earlier how Las Casas was conditioned by the Spanish culture. We have also seen that he was an eye-witness to the cruel treatment that his Spanish compatriots inflicted upon the natives. It remains, now, to highlight why this man of God could well be called the patron saint of interculturation.

In the tradition of the prophets Las Casas spoke truth to power, confronting the structures of injustice being perpetuated in the name of the Church and Spain. On May 20, in Santa Marta, (today, Columbia), Las Casas wrote a strong letter to the Spanish Emperor, Charles V. Excerpts

---

12. Ibid., 23.

are quoted here at some length to give the reader a deeper insight into the prophetic style and character of the saintly Las Casas:

> I submit, sacred Caesar (Charles V), that the remedy for the ills that beset this territory is that Your Majesty remove from positions of authority the cruel usurpers presently in control and entrust it to some one who will love and care for it as he would his own offspring and will treat it properly as it deserves, and that Your Majesty attend to this as a matter of highest priority. If nothing is done, I am certain that the whole territory will very soon simply disappear from the face of the earth, given the ways in which the cruel usurpers now maltreat and belabor it.[13]

It is important to note Las Casas' plea for "some one who will love and care ... as he would his own offspring"; there is no hint, in the words or feelings of Las Casas, of an inferior status being subscribed to the native peoples. From Las Casas' perspective, the native inhabitants have the same rights and dignity as the Spaniards. In his own way, Las Casas is defending the notion that the natives are entitled to the human rights that are God-given. The respect and reverence for the native cultures, as shown by Las Casas, is a prerequisite for true interculturation; in this, as in the vision of Las Casas, the two cultures should live side-by-side as equals.

While Las Casas agreed that, through the 'plenitude of papal power,' the pope could give away the lands of pagan princes, he also took a firm stand against the Spanish absolutist interpretation of papal power:

> Thus although the papal grant might confer sovereignty over the New World upon Catholic monarchs, it did not confer property rights over the persons or lands of its inhabitants. These, he insisted, remained theirs by natural right. Nor did it deprive the native rulers of their political authority ... The 'Kings' and 'princes' of the Americas enjoyed the same status as the nobility in Naples and Milan, both of which formed part of the Spanish Empire at this time.[14]

Significantly, in terms of prophetic ministry, Las Casas felt he had to oppose the expansion of papal power among the local peoples. Las Casas did so in view of the natural rights of the natives of the new world. Defending

---

13. Ibid., 81.
14. Ibid., xvi.

these natural rights was simply an application of scholastic Catholic teaching about the natural law, in which it was argued that God was the author of both natural and divine law. So, the dignity of the new culture was not dependent on the condescending generosity of the conquering country, but was always already there as constitutive of the dignity of the created world of God. Las Casas was clearly well-educated in the Catholic teaching on the natural law, and knew how to apply it in a totally new situation. The conquistadores, who were operating on an entirely different system of principles, had a prophet in their midst. But sadly, as often happens to prophets, his words of protest were not heeded in his own lifetime.

One of the great virtues of Las Casas' witness in the Americas is his great devotion in serving the truth as he saw it, giving no heed to the possible consequences to his own welfare. On every page of his book he appears ready to lay down his life for the truth. He does not mince words, lest he be misunderstood. Even in the Introduction to his account, Las Casas indicts with blistering words those involved in these horrific events:

> The reason the Christians have murdered on such a vast scale and killed everyone in their way is purely and simply greed. They have set out to line their pockets with gold and to amass private fortunes as quickly as possible so that they can then assume a status quite at odds with that into which they were born.[15]

In addition to the drive of greed in imperial politics, Las Casas was also quite aware of the power of the caste system in the Spanish culture. Thus, he did not hesitate to point out that the desire for status was also a contributing cause in the conquistadores' commission of unspeakable crimes against an innocent culture.

That Las Casas could be both bishop and prophet was a great blessing for the Church and especially for the native culture. His life is a powerful witness that, as Vatican II reminds us, the Church is called to heal and develop human cultures. The Church mediates the healing and redeeming grace of the risen Lord in every age and in every culture. That is its ministry to the world, the world for which the historical Jesus shed his blood.

---

15. Ibid., 13.

QUESTIONS FOR DISCUSSION

1. What parts of Bartolomé de las Casas' life apply to the process of inculturation today?
2. Do you ever "speak truth to power" like writing, or & mailing, your senators or mayor?
3. Can you detect any remnants of discrimination against the Latinos of today? In what forms?
4. Were you surprised that a pope at one time taught that the separation of Church and State was an error?
5. Do you think Bartolomé de las Casas should be canonized as a Saint? Why? Or why not?

9

Conclusions

WE ARE QUITE FAMILIAR with many new Church ministries such as lectors, Eucharistic ministers, Catechetical ministers, etc. The new ministerial situation in the Church is seen in the U.S. Bishops' wonderful statement on Lay Ecclesial Ministry called, "Co-workers in the Vineyard of the Lord," published in English and Spanish, December, 2005. But, we are not used to hearing about ministries to our culture; especially, we are perhaps unfamiliar with the ministries of diagnosing, healing, and developing our cultures. Yet, Chapter II of *The Pastoral Constitution on the Church in the Modern World*, from the Second Vatican Council, calls all the baptized to the mission of proper development of culture. That Vatican II understood this document—the commission—to be a *Constitution*, even labeling it so, undergirds the importance and the weight of its contents.

The purpose of this book is to activate a prayerful discernment process that may lead to a new kind ministry in the church. This ministry, like the ministry in Acts 6:1–6, will be new. While many of us have been active in the culture around us, we have not yet formally instituted ministries to our cultures. Even thinking about such a ministry may be scary and perplexing. We could easily dismiss the thought of such a task as an unreal or impossible dream. We could even invent a long list of excuses. However, as *The Pastoral Constitution on the Church in the Modern World* definitely teaches us, our culture is the product of human effort, and needs to be refined and developed. And this is the task appointed to us, which we are called out to perform since we have all been commissioned by our baptismal anointing into the common priesthood of the faithful. We are anointed to be the salt and yeast of the earth. Yeast, it should be remembered, is very active agent, and, without it, the dough remains dough, nothing more. So, we are called to be creative agents of change within our cultures.

This is a challenging vocation, especially given that we are now a multicultural country. We need to support the cultural diversity around us; at the same time, we need to be an active force for unity within the multiplicity of cultures. Our essential tasks are to nurture and cultivate the good, the wheat, in these new cultures; as well, we need to discern and heal the wounds, the weeds, in these cultures. So, concretely what can we do?

First, we know there is no such thing as a Lone Ranger ministry in the church. We can do a lot on our own, but we are sent by a specific Church community, and we are accountable to it. So, we need to start with our own parish pastoral council. We can ask the council to hold a special meeting devoted to prayerful discernment about the virtues and vices in the cultures within the local area. As a point of departure, consult chapters four and five, which will provide a foundation for engaging in a community diagnosis. Importantly, these things must be guided by prayer—invocation of the Spirit—and imaginative creativity. For example, in the course of evaluating the cultures with your own community, take a newspaper and a blackboard, and list the positive elements and the negative elements you discern, each in a single column. Then, by consensus, prioritize both lists in the order of importance. Now, you are ready to select those items that correspond to the particular talents or ministries of the people in the Church. Agree to report back to the council in six months. This is one instance of how we hold ourselves accountable for our ministries.

Second, like Bishop Bartolomé de las Casas, speak truth to power. Write letters or e-mails to your senators, representatives, mayors, and city council about Christian issues, like immigration, peace-making, or health care reform. Join up with bloggers and make your voice heard. Get on a bus and join the 22,000 students who stage a protest, on November 19, at The School of the Americas in Georgia. You will be one more voice protesting the violence, the tortures, the rapes, and the killings committed in Latin America by American trained soldiers. You will be the oil that heals some of the violence in our militaristic culture.

Above all, vote and volunteer to help with political campaigns. Where *you* are involved, politics will become a little less corrupt. Politics, according to Webster, is the art or science of government; so, as a U.S. citizen, you belong there. Being active and involved in the political process is a crucial part of refining and developing our political culture. The whole world is the Lord's vineyard for ministry, but, we must keep in mind, the world begins in our own backyard. When the pallbearers carry our bodies to the

Conclusions

cemetery, the seeds of the Gospel we planted in our lifetime will continue to grow, even after we are gone. We plant the seeds *with our lives and actions*, and it is "God [who] will make it grow" (1 Cor 3:6).

There are at least a million other ways in which we can develop the multiculturalism of our society. Our sensitivity to the Spirit and our own creativity will open new vistas, new doors, for our ministries. God can and does use unlikely subjects like us—God does the choosing, not according to our finite thoughts, but according to His own. Even more, God uses our talents, abilities, and actions for good in ways we unaware of and for purposes we may never know; we must always be mindful that "My thoughts are not your thoughts, nor are your ways my ways, says the Lord" (Is 55:8).

A final word about parishes. The Church is more organism than organization, just as Paul calls it a body. As such, it responds to human organisms like us. We ourselves are the anointed, living sacraments through which the Holy Spirit will renew the face of the earth. We may, at times, be overcome by fear at the awesome task ahead of us, but our vocation calls us. And it is the Lord's strength, not our own, that will propel us onward. The Lord's love is a power way beyond our own understanding. And ministry, especially in its outcomes, remains a mystery. When we are stricken by fear, we can recall those immortal words of Francis Thompson:

"Fear wist not to evade as Love wist to pursue."

From *The Hound of Heaven*

Appendix I

AÑORANZA

Por Elida Rademacher

Vagan en el firmamento, los recuerdos del ayer,
Que fueron gloria y desencanto,
Que dejaron en mi alma soñadora,
Memorias imborrables, de aquella vida mía.
    Recuero a mi bella y frágil madre,
    Cuidándonos con su amor cada día,
    La ardua vida de mi padre,
    Con su admirable inteligencia,
    Nos enseño el trabajo desde niños,
    Y a no desfallecer, ante las durezas de la vida.
Recuero a la dulce abuela,
Llevándome de la mano, yo con un sombrerito antiguo,
Presurosas, a la misa, las campanas repicando,
Sus sabios consejos, que iluminaron mi vida,
Su amor y los años felices que pasé a su lado.
    Las jugarretas de mi niñez en la escuela,
    Las lecciones de memoria,
    El gua a la hora de recreo,
    Las amigas que no olvido,
    La vieja campana de la escuela,
    Su eco me parece tan lejano.
El viejo reloj de la torre,
Las antiguas campanas de la Iglesia
Resonando en los altos Cuchumatanes,
Que le cantara el poeta, Juan Dieguez Olaverri,
El paseo al mirador, el Cerrito de la Cruz,

Appendix I

El Calvario en la colina,
Las caminatas al llano grande y buenos aires,
La Laguna de Ocubila, llena de algas,
El paseo al frío Río San Juan en Aguacatán,
Los rregadillos, y su misteriosa campana en la pradera,
La presa grande, el hoyo oscuro,
Con salida al viejo molino,
Los días de campo, bajo los árboles,
Caminando por el río,
Contemplando las pinedas.

    Las calles empedradas, de mi Chiantla querida,
    Donde descalza, en los ríos
    Con mis hermanos y amiguitos, jugueteábamos,
    Después de los grandes aguaceros.
    Los domingos en el Kiosco del parque viejo,
    Escuchábamos nuestra Marimba Kaibil Balam.
Las Ferias de Candelaria y Natividad,
Los achimeros, con sus ventas,
Con trastecitos de barro, carritos de madera,
Muñecas de trapo,
Jugábamos de niños y éramos felices,
Las ventas del dulce Alfinique de Sacapulas,
El mazapán y las rosquitas,
El rico algodón de colores,
Los pajaritos de la buena suerte,
Las loterías de premio daban vasitos,
La rueda de caballitos dando vueltecitas,
Al compás de su marimbita con el mismo sonecito.
    En el atrio de la Iglesia
    Lleno de cofrades, con el tambor y la chirimía,
    Quemando candelas e incienso,
    Con romero y rosarios,
    Los romeristas, pidiéndole milagros a la Virgen.
Al final de la feria,
Con bombas y cohetes,
Llevan en hombros a la virgencita llena de flores,

Appendix I

En procesión van los fieles devotos,
Los romeristas y cofradías.
Algunos van rezando, todos van cantando
Los alabados con la misma melodía
Bajo el sol fulgurante de medio día.
    Cuantas memorias guardo en mi corazón,
    Las que jamás volveré a vivir,
    Y ahora con mi cabeza cana y triste,
    Allanando con mis lágrimas la distancia,
    De lo que quisiera volver a mirar.

YEARNING

By Elida Rademacher

They wander in the firmament, the memories of my yester year,
They were glory and disenchantment
That left in my dreaming soul,
Indelible memories, of that life of mine.
    I remember my beautiful and fragile mother,
    Taking care of us each day with her love,
    The arduous life of my father,
    With his admirable intelligence,
    Who taught us as children to work,
    And to faint not, before the hardness of life.
I remember my sweet grandmother,
Taking me by the hand, me, in a petite old-fashioned hat,
Walking hastily to Mass, the bells clanging,
Her wise counsels that illuminated my life,
Her love and the blissful years that I spent by her side.
    The mischievous tricks of my childhood at school,
    The lessons by memory,
    The snacks at recess time,
    The girlfriends that I shall never forget,
    The old school bell,
    Its echo seems so distant to me.
The old tower clock,
The antique bells of the Church,

Appendix I

Echoing in the tall Cuchumatanes Mountains,
To which the poet Juan Dieguez Olaverri sang,
The stroll to the vantage point, the Hill of the Cross,
The Calvary on the hill,
The hikes to the large flat and the village,
The Lagoon of Ocubila, filled of algae,
The stroll to the cold river of San Juan in Aguacatán,
The village or "Los Rregadillos" and its mysterious bell in the Meadow,
The large dam, the dark pit,
With an exit towards the old mill,
The picnics under the trees,
Walking by the river,
Contemplating the pine trees.

    The cobblestone streets, of my beloved Chiantla,
    Where barefoot, in the rivers,
    With my siblings and friends, we frolicked
    After the heavy rainstorms.
    Sundays in the gazebo of the old park,
    We listened to our Marimba Kaibil Balam.
The Festival of Lights and Nativity,
The peddlers, with their sales,
Dishes of clay, wooden cars, rag dolls,
We played as children and were joyful,
The sales of the sweets Alfinique of Sacapulas,
The marzipan and the rosquitas,
The delicious and colorful cotton candy,
The tiny birds of good luck,
The lotteries which awarded small drinking glasses as prizes,
The large wheel with the fastened miniature ponies circling around
To the beat of their miniature marimba with the same rhythm.
    In the vestibule of the Church
    Filled with worshippers, with the drum and the shawm,
    Burning candles and incense,
    With rosemary and rosaries,
    The pilgrims, asking for miracles from the Virgin.
At the end of the festival,

Appendix I

With fireworks and rockets,
They carry on shoulders the Virgin surrounded with flowers.
In procession they go, the faithful devotees,
The pilgrims and worshippers,
Some go praying, all go singing
The praises with the same melody
Under the glittering sun of midday.
    So many memories I keep in my heart,
    The ones I will never live again,
    And now with my gray hair, and saddened,
    Quietly contemplating with my tears the distance
    Of what I would like to see once again.

                        Translation by Angelica A. Webster

Appendix II

Theology and the Indigenous Cultures of the Americas: Conditions of Dialogue

A ONE-SIDED DIALOGUE BETWEEN DR. MARÍA PILAR AQUINO AND DR. WILLIAM J. RADEMACHER.

What follows is a selection of excerpts from Dr. María Pilar Aquino's excellent essay delivered at the 61st Convention of the Catholic Theological Society of America in San Antonio on June 8, 2006. The excerpts, in my judgment, enhance several chapters in this book, and, at the same time, break some new ground with respect to the emerging theologies of the indigenous cultures of the Americas. It is my hope that the publication of parts of Aquino's work in conjunction with multiculturalism will give her fine piece a wider exposure, and may also encourage readers to read the whole essay as published in CTSA Proceedings in Vol. 61 (2006).

In the first section, I will provide an excerpt from Dr. Aquino's article, and then I will add my own commentary, as a simple dialogue. Following this, which serves as example of how the dialogue will proceed throughout the rest of this appendix, I will provide lengthier segments from her article, interspersed with my commentary, which will be marked for the reader. This engagement is as an effort to make a connection between Aquino's commendable work, especially her concern for ecclesial attention to native cultures, with various parts of my own book. Our dialogue will be a little unfair since it is a one-sided response with excerpts chosen out of context primarily in view of their positive relation to themes developed at some length in my own book. Besides, I chose these particular excerpts precisely because I find myself totally in agreement with them.

Appendix II

I fondly hope readers will take the time to read Dr. Aquino's whole essay. They will be richly rewarded for their extra effort.

William J. Rademacher

1. EXCERPT FROM AQUINO'S TEXT ...

From the tradition of Catholic Christianity, the theological and missiological works developed over a period of nearly forty years by C. Starkloff represent both a rich legacy and a vision for an interactive conversation between Christianity and Native American religions. From his pioneer book *The People of the Center*,[1] published more than thirty years ago, to his challenging, latest work *A Theology of the In-Between: The Value of Syncretic Process*,[2] his contribution has been valued by a new generation of Catholic scholars as being thoughtful and creative, careful and effective, as well as dynamic and courageous.[3] Studies made on the history of United States Catholicism appear to be more abundant, but some of these studies address the Indigenous communities only as they are pertinent to understand the colonial times of the United States Church.[4] From the distinctive framework of systematic theology, the book *Christ is a Native American*[5] by A. Peelman, an Oblate priest from Canada, represents a pioneering work in the theological dialogue between Christian faith and Amerindian cultures in the context of the Canadian Indian Christian communities. From the perspective of United States Latino/a Theology, the works of Ana María Pineda have been consistent in engaging the

---

1. Carl F. Starkloff, *The People of the Center American Indian Religion and Christianity* (New York: Seabury Press, 1974).

2. Carl F. Starkloff, *A Theology of the In-Between: The Value of Syncretic Process* (Milwaukee: Marquette University Press, 2002).

3. Mark S. Clatterbuck, "Post Vatican II Inculturation among Native North American Catholics: A Study in the Missiology of Father Carl Starkloff, S.J.," *Missiology: An International Review* 31/2 (April 2003): 207-22.

4. See, e.g., James J. Hennessey, *American Catholics: A History of the Roman Catholic Community in the United States* (New York: Oxford University Press, 1981); Jay P. Dolan, *The American Catholic Experience. A History from the Colonial Times to the Present* (Garden City, NY: Doubleday, 1985); Suzanne Hall, ed., *The People: Reflections of Native Peoples on the Catholic Experience in North America* (Washington, DC: National Catholic Educational Association, 1992); Chester Gillis, *Roman Catholicism in America* (New York: Columbia University Press, 1999); James T. Fisher, *Communion of Immigrants: A History of Catholics in America* (New York: Oxford University Press, 2000); Patrick W. Carey, *Catholics in America: A History* (Westport, CT: Praeger Publishers, 2004).

5. Achiel Peelman, *Christ Is a Native American* (Maryknoll NY: Orbis Books, 1995).

Appendix II

worldview of Mesoamerican religious traditions, especially those that gather *la palabra antigua* (the ancient word).[6] Other than these, I failed to find other systematic approaches elaborated by United States Catholic theologians. Therefore, I have reached the conclusion that, from the stand point of the Catholic Christian tradition, Indigenous theologies are insufficiently systematized.

COMMENTARY 1

Theology, if it is to serve the people of God, does indeed need to be systematized. It is up to theologians to find the story, or to create a system, a language, and framework through which the Word of God, while remaining a saving Word, is passed on from one generation to the next. After the Council of Trent (1545-1563), Catholic theology was organized as a system to defend the truths of revelation against the Protestants. Official theology books with an *imprimatur* contained the theology designed to defend both the truth and the Church teaching that truth. Written in unchangeable Latin in a thesis format, these theological manuals represented a canonized system for teaching and learning theology. And, we have to admit, these theology textbooks were born and raised in the European West. They were shaped in a defensive mode. This theology came totally "from above." So the deductive method became the norm. There is no hint in this system of any influence from the rich Asian, African or Amerindian cultures.

Yet the historical Jesus was a Jew. The God-man became enfleshed in a Jewish culture. So, if theology is going to proclaim a saving Word, it has to do so within a specific culture. And it has to listen first to that culture's unique story. Every culture has its very own story. It shapes that culture and at the same time calls it to a higher destiny.

The Jesus story of pain and suffering may be part of that culture's own story. It may be a mirror of the Jesus story. So theology has to ask, how does the Jesus story fit into this culture's story. It's clear, as Dr. Aquino has shown , that we have not yet developed systematic indigenous theologies which speak words of life to the Asian, Indian, or African stories. *Teología*

---

6. See especially Ana María Pineda, "Evangelization of the "New World": A New World Perspective," *Missiology: An international Review* 20/2 (April 1992): 151–61; Ana Maria Pineda, "The Oral Tradition of a People: Forjadora de Rostro y Corazón," in *Hispanic/Latino Theology. Challenge and Promise*, ed. Ada María Isasi-Díaz and Fernando F. Segovia (Minneapolis: Fortress Press, 1996) 104–16.

Appendix II

India emerges from the life of the community. Thus it is a theology "from below." But it is also a theology "from above." If it is true *Teología India*, it is incarnate in a particular community. But that is not the end. With its continuing incarnation It remains *Theos*=God and *Logos*=Word. That is, it also has a transcendent dimension whereby it is always linked to the life-giving God "from above." Thus, it is shaped by the Word "from above," and the incarnation "from below." We recognize *Teología India* as distinct primarily through its incarnation "from below." The life in the community, of course, includes the blood and sweat in the field and factory. It is not restricted to the spiritual. There is no dualism in the life of the community, dividing *Teologia India* into the sacred "from above" and the secular "from below." Thus *Teologia India* is never static. It is always receiving new life "from above" and being transformed both "from above" and from its new incarnations "from below." Its distinct identity as *Teologia India* does not imply separation from the universal Church or its theology. On the contrary, it is nourished by that theology and, at the same time, it adds a new and unique life-giving dimension to it. It is like a branch on the tree, giving and receiving life at the same time.

2. AQUINO'S TEXT...

Contitions Contributing to the Emergence of Teologia India

In *Teología India,* the function of the theologian is described as one of acting as scriveners, as amanuensis, as notaries or recorders, and as postal carriers.[7] The Náhuatl language uses the word *Tlacuilo/a* to describe this function. That is why Indigenous theologian E. López Hernández presents himself as functioning as a *Tlacuilo* or scrivener of the community.[8] The theologian, who can be Indigenous or non-Indigenous, has the function of systematizing the religious visions, understandings and practices of the people, and to communicate or deliver them to other communities and to the broader world. This is so, because a key presupposition of *Teología India* is that the subjects of theological elaboration are the communities

---

7. Aiban Wagua, "Las Teologías Indias ante la Globalidad de la Teología Cristiana," in *Teología India. Primer Encuentro Taller Latinoamericano,*" ed. Eleazar López Hernández (México: Centro Nacional de Ayuda a las Misiones Indígenas and Abya Yala, 1991) 300; Eleazar López Hernández, *Teología India. Antología,* 25.

8. López Hernández, *Teología India. Antología,* 25.

Appendix II

themselves. These are communities who together share, reflect, and articulate their faith experiences as subjects of thought and action.[9] Theology flows from the living faith of communities who foster religious languages in view of supporting processes that actualize hope, human dignity, celebration, justice, and liberation. That is why the subjects of theology are considered to be "subjects in transformation."[10]

Although professional theologians assist the communities in the critical and scientific articulation of theological language, they do not replace the community as the primary subject of theology.[11] According to Ana María Pineda, "it was crucial that the *tlacuilo* know the symbols of mythology and tradition ... The *tlacuilo* was the master of the visual communication of the communal history of the *pueblo*."[12] In the process of doing *Teología India* it is often difficult to say who said what because, in spite of the plurality of expressions, the Indigenous communities maintain significant commonalities in terms of their deeply communitarian or collective ways of elaborating thought. They produce highly refined syntheses of their interpretation of how God, the God of Four Hundred Names, The Heart of Heaven and Heart of Earth, that is the Infinite God,[13] is present and active in their midst.

COMMENTARY 2

That the theologian is a mere scrivener may be a little shocking to those who do not know what is meant by a Systematic Theology which emerges from the life of the community. This theology, in so far as the Word be-

---

9. López Hernández, ed., Teología India. Primer Encuentro Taller Latinoamericano, 261–62, 315.

10. López Hernández, ed., Teología India. Primer Encuentro Taller Latinoamericano, 262.

11. Petul Cut Chab, "Conceptos Básicos de la Teología India Mayense," in *Sabiduría Indígena. Fuente de Esperanza. Teología India II Parte Aportes. III Encuentro-Taller Latinoamericano (Cochabamba Bolivia, 24 a! 30 de agosto de 1997)*, ed. Gisela Grundges, (Cusco, Perú: Instituto de Estudios Aymaras IDEA-Perú, Centro de Teología Popular CTP Bolivia, Instituto de Pastoral Andina IPA-Perú, 1998) 185–87.

12. Ana Maria Pineda, "The Oral Tradition of a People," 108–9.

13. Centro Nacional de Ayuda a las Misiones Indigenas de México, "Flores de México," in *Sabiduría Indigena. Fuente de Esperanza. Teología India IlParte Aportes. IllEncuentro-Taller Latinoamericano, Cochabaniba, Bolivia, 24 al 30 de agosto de 1997*, ed. Gisela Grundges (Cusco, Perú: Instituto de Estudios Aymaras IDEA-Perú, Centro de Teología Popular CTP-Bolivia, Instituto de Pastoral Andina IPA-Perú, 1998) 113–14.

comes incarnate, comes from the community and belongs to it. So, the theologian has to remain the community's scrivener. He or she is not the originator of the community's theology, even though one may give it a systematic form. As a scrivener, he or she performs an important task in sharing the community's theology with other communities and with the universal Church. The scrivener also exercises the gift of discernment, since theology does not emerge from the community in a pure form. In view of the long tradition of the universal theology, one can sift the wheat from the chaff while providing a systematic form to the community's theology. The Word of God is *of* God; but it is also *of* the human.

3. AQUINO TEXT . . .

The strength and vitality of *Teología India* in contemporary times is the result of many factors that have come together to bring forth the forces and possibilities contained in reality itself.[14] One factor of great significance, that represents a commonality running across every theology of liberation, is the refusal by the traditionally marginalized people to continue being considered as disposable objects or as mere recipients of somebody else's wicked purposes. For the Indigenous communities, this refusal has meant that they no longer remain silent in the face of oppressive systems and elite power groups that have imposed upon them a politics of submission coupled with a politics of assimilation for far too long. In the context of the emergence of the theologies of liberation during the second half of the twentieth century, *Teología India* came to light from a clandestine existence. The notion of the poor and marginalized as subjects of their own historical processes provided opportunities to assert that the Indigenous communities not only conceptualized themselves as subjects of society and culture, but also of the churches and of the theologies that inform their lives. The theological understandings that had been refined for centuries through the intercultural conversations of Indigenous faith and Christian faith, finally saw the light of day. Bishop G. López Reyes, of the Diocese of Verapaz, Guatemala, explains that "this theological project, as a struggle for the dignity and rights of the oppressed and marginalized people, inscribes itself within the theological thought that is expressed in

---

14. On the forces that intervene in historical processes, see Ellacuría, *Filosofía de la Realidad Histórica*, 447–57.

Appendix II

different forms in Latin America, and gives a special breath to the documents of Medellín, Puebla, and Santo Domingo.[15]

Along these lines, another factor that accounts for the growth of *Teología India* is that it has earned the respect and support of many Catholic bishops, priests, and theologians. In spite of stressful conditions imposed upon them by the higher authorities of the Catholic Church, many bishops have provided encouragement and means so that this theological perspective unfolds its roots in the diocesan environment. Prominent among these bishops are well-known names, such as Don Samuel Ruiz, Don Arturo Lona, Don Raúl Vera, Don Alvaro Ramazzini, Don Julio Cabrera Ovalle, including the great figures of deceased bishops such as Don Bartolomé Carrasco, also known as the "Bishop of the Poor," who was until 1999 the Fifth Archbishop of Oaxaca, Mexico, and Don José Llaguno Farías, S.J., who was until 1992, a prominent spokesperson of *Teología India* from his diocese in the Tarahumara Sierras of Chihuahua, Mexico.

A third factor that has highlighted the relevance of *Teología India* is the increasing impact and visibility of the current struggles of the Indigenous people in many countries such as Brasil, Mexico, Equador, Bolivia, Paraguay, Guatemala, and others. In this panorama, the Church is confronted with the need of providing a pastoral and a theological response to the struggles for human rights of the Amerindian people in terms of the demands of the people, not in terms of the interests of the ecclesiastical institution.

A fourth factor that I want to mention is the role of the ecumenical community in organizing congresses and symposia at both continental and national levels to advance the frameworks of *Teología India*. On this, the work of the Latin American Ecumenical Articulation of Indigenous Pastoral (Articulação Ecumênica Latino-Americana de Pastoral Indígena, AELAPI), and the Ecumenical Association of Third World Theologians (EATWOT) are worth mentioning. However, many other Church organizations are increasingly supporting and adopting the perspectives of *Teología India*, such as the Latin American Confederation of Religious Communities (Confederación Latinoamericana de Religiosos, CLAR), the Latin American Council of Churches (Consejo Latinoamericano de Iglesias, CLAI), and also the Latin American Conference of Bishops (Conferencia del Episcopado Latinoamericano, CELAM), and some

---

15. Mons. Gerardo Flores Reyes, "Aspectos Importantes de la Teología India," in *Sabiduría Indígena. Fuente de Esperanza. Teología India II Parte Aportes*, 239.

Appendix II

members of the International Association of Catholic Missiologists (IACM, Asociación Internacional de Misiólogos Católicos). But other organizations directly connected to the work of the Catholic Church have also played a significant role in the growing vitality and impact of *Teología India,* such as the National Center of Assistance to Indigenous Missions (Centro Nacional de Ayuda a las Misiones Indígenas, CENAMI, Mexico); the Missionary Indigenous Council (Conselho Indigenista Missionário, CIMI, Brasil); the Pastoral Andean Institute (Instituto de Pastoral Andina, IPA, Perú); the Center of Popular Theology (Centro de Teología Popular, CTP, Bolivia); the National Coordination of Indigenous Pastoral (Coordinadora Nacional de Pastoral Indígena, CONAPI, Panama), and *Amerindia,* a significant group of theological and pastoral experts . At the time of this writing, the most recent continental encounter of *Teología India* took place this past April 21–26, 2006 in Manaus, Brazil.

Given these developments, I can safely say that today, the majority of Latin American Catholic theologians are aware that we cannot continue doing theology without engaging in a serious conversation with *Teología India.* These amazing and challenging developments could not have been predicted at the time of the Second Vatican council.

COMMENTARY 3

In our own time the poor and marginalized have decided they no longer need to accept the status of victims of structured power systems. They have decided they can indeed be masters of their own destiny both in the Church and in society. After all, there are many instances in the bible where salvation means liberation. The Jewish exodus from a slave condition in Egypt is just one of many signs that oppressed peoples do not need "to remain silent in the face of oppressive systems."

The movement toward liberation within *Teología India* received considerable support from indigenous priests and bishops. This was a great blessing for *Teología India* while many European theologians were being silenced for breaking out of the Tridentine mold of doing theology. So with the support of some clergy and the missionary theology of Vatican II *Teologia India* is taking its well deserved place among the emerging, post-conciliar theologies.

Appendix II

4. AQUINO TEXT ...

For dialogue to take place, a key premise is the mutual recognition of the equality of the parties involved, and validation of the common interest that brings together equal partners in conversation. In the theological environment, dialogue is also a process in which diverse voices exchange their truths for the purpose of growing together in trust and in sincerity. Dialogue allows equal partners not just to know each other, but to learn together how to share a peaceful and a useful existence in common. For a United States Native American theology, dialogue is necessary so that "Indian people can speak as equals to Christians."[16] As for *Teología India*, dialogue is a term that runs across the different gatherings and written works, but the Third Latin American Encounter of *Teología India* that took place in 1997 is especially enlightening. At this Encounter, the participants agreed that dialogue "is a horizontal communication between equal and different people who share lived experiences, knowledge and expressions for mutual enrichment.

For dialogue to occur, it is necessary to recognize the other person as different, not as superior or inferior."[17] In their view, the Amerindian understanding of dialogue differs from the dominant Western-European understanding of dialogue in that, while the latter approaches dialogue through conceptual speculation for demonstrating their truths, the former approaches dialogue through exchange of life experiences that show common truths in the witness of life. Here, the two terms used in the Spanish language are "demostrar" (to demonstrate) and "mostrar" (to show, to exhibit). Therefore, for them, dialogue requires a shift from the abstract "demostrar" to the concrete "mostrar."[18] Theologically, conditions of dialogue entail the capacity of recognizing the partners in dialogue as equals, as well as horizontal communication and entering into a new space of trust where the different languages of faith are recognized as carriers of truth, as revelations of the many faces of God. Dialogue is not the unilateral delivery of a compendium of speculative truths but a life

---

16. Kidwell, Noley, and Tinker, *A Native American Theology*, 1.

17. Ramiro Argandoña, Diego Irarrázabal, and María José Caram Padilla, eds., Sabiduría Indígena. Fuente de Esperanza. Teología India II Parte Memoria. III Encuentro-Taller *Latinoamericano (Cochabamba, Bolivia, 24 al 30 de agosto de 1997)* (Cusco, Perú: Instituto de Estudios Aymaras IDEA-Perú, Centro de Teología Popular CTP-Bolivia, Instituto de Pastoral Andina IPA-Perú, 1998) 82.

18. Argandoña, Irarrázabal, and Padilla, *Sabiduría Indígena*, 83.

Appendix II

attitude, a framework and a process for learning how to live together in a peaceful and useful Christian existence.

COMMENTARY 4

Dialogue has been rather thoroughly discussed in Chapter three. But few understand the need for periods of silence to process the feelings words cannot convey. And, most of the time, the feelings are more important than the words. This is especially true with men who find it hard to share their feelings. Non-judgmental listening is a difficult art to learn. But until we learn it, true dialogue is impossible. Bushels of words can stumble along. But there is no communication until ideas and feelings are actually received.

5. AQUINO TEXT . . .

The core principle sustaining the "autochthonous" churches is provided by *Ad Gentes* in its understanding of the whole Church as becoming missionary for the fullness of Christian life: "As members of the living Christ . . . all the children of the church should have a lively consciousness of their responsibility for the world, they should foster within themselves a truly catholic spirit, they should spend themselves in the work of the gospel. However, let everyone be aware that the primary and most important contribution they can make to the spread of the faith is to lead a profound Christian life."[19] In the context of the "autochthonous" churches there is an intense activity of critical analysis of the oppressive and dehumanizing structures of society and church that prevent the actualization of the truth of the Gospel. That is why, in this context, the notion of an "integrated evangelization"[20] is crucial, as it involves the work of the Church in restoring the values and dignity of the human person, strengthening the resources and ministries of the communities, and implementing operative means for change and transformation from within the symbols, myths, and rituals of the Indigenous communities.

---

19. Second Vatican Council, *Decree on the Church's Missionary Activity Ad Gentes Divinitus*, in A. Flannery, 489. As opposed to the version of *Ad Gentes* published by the Holy See, I prefer to use Flannery's version because of its formulation in inclusive language.

20. Msgr. Raúl Vera López, "Comentario a las Exposiciones Acerca de la Situación de los Pueblos Mayas," in *Teología India Mayense II. Memorias, Experiencias y Reflexiones de Encuentros Teológicos Regionales*, ed. Centro Nacional de Ayuda a las Misiones Indígenas (México: Centro Nacional de Ayuda a las Misiones Indígenas, 1998) 38–39.

Appendix II

The "autochthonous" churches develop processes aimed at communicating life and hope to those who seek God's wisdom to find ways for shaping a better future together. *Teología India* finds its roots in the lived experiences, in the critical reflection, and in the transforming dynamics of the "autochthonous" churches. Both are expressions of the Church, and both trace their breath to the life-giving impulses of *Ad Gentes*. Particularly important for the development of "autochthonous" churches are the insights *of Ad Gentes,* such as: support of the "autochthonous" particular churches that grow out of the seeds of the word of God, that should be adequately organized and possess their own energy and maturity (n. 6); endowed with the cultural riches of their nations, these churches should be deeply rooted in the people (n. 15);

COMMENTARY 5

Indigenous Churches remain the ideal. But realistically they continue to be a dream. Without priests there is no Eucharist; and without the Eucharist there is no Church. But it is still important to keep the dream alive. Dreams help us get up in the morning. They take us beyond the ordinary. That Dr. Martin Luther King, in spite of overwhelming odds, could cling to his dream, is a mark of his greatness. We celebrate the dream as well as the man. Eucharistic presiders presently come "from above." No doubt the power of the Holy Spirit, always present in the Church will soon be unleashed to solve the crisis which is of human origin. The shortage of priests is a disciplinary problem. It can be solved by humans who have a vision of what the Church can become. That vision includes the birth of thousands of "autochthonous" Churches. The crisis, as Dr. Aquino describes it, is extremely urgent. Thousands of churches are ready to "heal and develop" our wounded cultures. They have been silent for centuries. But, no more. They are quite aware of Vatican II's document, "*Ad Gentes*." Their voices will get louder as the years go on. Through them the Church will experience a New Pentecost.

6. AQUINO TEXT ...

First, there are more than fifty million indigenous people across the Americas who speak more than 500 different languages. They are neither the remnant of an extinguished people or insignificant minorities.

Appendix II

They have not been annihilated but represent the most consistent human population in the midst of an evolving society.

Second, although they are the most impoverished population of the Americas, the progress and survival of humanity and of the earth depend largely on our ability to connect with the sifted wisdom, community structure and organizational methods that the Indigenous people have cultivated through the centuries for the healing and caring of all.

Third, while contemporary cultures and societies are denying God's presence in the human through their subjugation of others, the Indigenous people have affirmed their deep connection to God through their struggles for human rights.

Fourth, the Indigenous people are not opposed to Christian faith, nor are they enemies of the Church. It is not they who have rejected the Gospel of Jesus Christ nor they who have occluded the transforming presence and activity of God's Holy Spirit in their midst. Avoiding false idealizations and acknowledging in them the many limitations that still need to be overcome, the Indigenous communities strongly assert that to be Christians and to perform ecclesial ministries, the Church must cease to consider them idolaters in need of conversion to the true faith and to expect them to renounce their ancestral religions traditions. Such expectation only accomplishes the denial of their self-realization as humans and leads to make of them schizophrenic people who are forced to use masks to cover up their true selves as Christians and as humans. In their view, purification of wicked ways, conversion to the truth of the Gospel, and dedication to work for the Reign of God, are demands that Christian faith raises for the whole Church.

Fifth, the indigenous communities recognize that, having self-preservation in mind, for centuries they have maintained a prudent silence within the churches. Empowered by Christ's message, however, such an attitude has been replaced across the Americas by courage and audacity to continue their work in the renewal of the Church and in the historical advancement of God's Reign. Respectful communication between equals, sincere and trustful dialogue is what they offer to the Church and what they expect to receive from the Church's leadership.

One final issue of this document that I found to be most inspiring is the strong affirmation of social and ecclesial reconciliation as a goal that the Indigenous communities seek to achieve. In their view, reconciliation is an urgent task for all in the Church, so that we come together in a com-

Appendix II

mitment to build a different future in which the harms done by the Church in the past against the Indigenous communities, are not repeated again. In their view, reconciliation in the Church also requires that the Church's leadership publicly refutes the notion that the Amerindian Christian communities are second-class Christians or incomplete Catholics. This requires a formal acknowledgment of the truthfulness and authenticity of the "autochthonous" churches, ministries and theologies. In support of this view, the Indigenous communities assert that the message of St. Paul to the Corinthians is again actualized to the letter in them:

> [I]n everything we commend ourselves as ministers of God, through much endurance, in afflictions, hardships, constraints, beatings, imprisonments, riots, labors, vigils, fasts; . . . in truthful speech, in the power of God; with weapons of righteousness at the right and at the left; through glory and dishonor, insult and praise. We are treated as deceivers and yet are truthful; as unrecognized and yet acknowledged; as dying and behold we live; as chastised and yet not put to death; as sorrowful yet always rejoicing; as poor yet enriching many; as having nothing and yet possessing all things. (2 Cor 6:4–10 NAB)

COMMENTARY 6

This is probably the most powerful section in the whole essay. "Fifty million indigenous people" present a missionary challenge that should engage the whole Church day and night. It is only right that Dr. Aquino should emphasize the need for reconciliation. In Chapter Three we got a glimpse of the genocide these Latino peoples have suffered with the help and blessing of the Christian Church. It is most important that we name the sin and suffer the shame that goes with it. Then, and only then, will we be ready for the reconciliation with the thousands of indigenous communities. Too long have they suffered. And too long have they been ignored by the Church. But now their voices are becoming a great shout across the land. We will embrace them with a penitential kiss of peace; or, there will be an invasion like we have never seen before. Myriads of fences and human laws will not stop a people whose sweat and blood has been exploited for hundreds of years. Both our Church and our country will be richer for their presence. They have been purified by the fires of hell; now they are ready to purify their Church and their adopted country.

Appendix II

7. AQUINO TEXT ...

On the issue of affirming the Christian religious experience of Amerindians today, the insight of C. Starkloff remains valid. Over thirty years ago, he suggested that Christian theology can be most valuable as it assists in the liberation processes of Amerindians "by finally confessing to the dignity of those traditions ... for a sense of one's own history is part of the sense of personal and communal dignity, which liberates through equalization."[21] Accordingly, the authenticity of Christian faith and the universality of the Church cannot be affirmed through the unilateral enforcement of centralizing, romanocentric theological frameworks and religious practices. For Catholic Christianity to affirm its universal existence, the leadership of the Church must recognize, rather than suppress, the truth of the faith rooted in the concrete realities of Indigenous Christians. Theologically, this is a universality that flows from the common living out of the mystery of God revealed by Jesus Christ in the plural contexts of today's world. In other terms, the life itself of "autochthonous" churches is a radical demand of the universality of the Church because they flow from its inner nature. By acknowledging and supporting the culturally embodied churches, as eloquently shown by the existing "autochthonous" churches and *Teología India*, Catholic Christianity asserts both the authenticity and universality of its evangelizing mission.

Dr. María Pilar Aquino
University of San Diego
San Diego, California

---

21. Starkloff, *The People of the Center*, 134.

Bibliography

Books

Aquinas, St. Thomas. *Summa Theologica*. 5 volumes. Translated by Fathers of the English Dominican Province. New York: Benziger Bros, 1947.
Armstrong, Karen. *Muhammad: A Prophet for Our Time*. New York: HarperCollins, 2006.
———. *Islam: A Short History*. New York: Random House, 2002.
———. *Holy War: The Crusades and Their Impact on Today's World*. 2nd ed. New York: Anchor Books, 2001.
Augustine, St. *The City of God*. Translated by Henry Bettenson. New York: Penguin, 1972.
Bacevich, Andrew. *The New American Militarism: How Americans Are Seduced by War*. New York: Oxford University Press, 2005.
———. *American Empire: The Realities and Consequences of U. S. Diplomacy*. Cambridge: Harvard University Press, 2002.
Baranowski, Arthur. *Pastoring the Pastors*. Cincinnati, OH: St. Anthony Messenger Press, 1988.
Boorstin, Daniel. *The Seekers: The Story of Man's Continuing Quest to Understand His World*. New York: Random House, 1998.
Boys, Mary C., ed. *Seeing Judaism Anew*. New York: Rowman & Littlefield Publishers, 2005.
Brockey, Liam Matthew. *Journey to the East: The Jesuit Mission to China, 1579-1724*. 2007.
Bullard, Robert, ed. *The Quest for Environmental Justice: Human Rights and the Politics of Pollution*. San Francisco: Sierra Club Books, 2005.
Cantor, Norman. *The Civilization of the Middle Ages*. New York: HarperPerennial, 1994.
Carey, Patrick W. *Catholics in America: A History*. Westport, CT: Praeger Publishers, 2004.
Catechism of the Catholic Church. Libera Editrice Vaticana. Translated and edited by the United States Catholic Conference. Ligouri, MO: Liguori Press, 1994.
The Catholic Encyclopedia. 19 volumes. Edited by the Faculty of the Catholic University of America. New York: McGraw-Hill: 1967-1995.
Chavez, Linda. *Out of the Barrio: Toward a New Politics of Hispanic Assimilation*. New York: Basic Books, 1991.
Cottingham, John. *Rationalism*. Paladin Movements and Ideas. Edited by Justin Wintle. London: Paladin, 1997.
de las Casas, Bartolomé. *The Devastation of the Indies*. Translated by Herman Briffault Baltimore: Johns Hopkins University, 1992.
Ernst, Carl. *Following Muhammad: Rethinking Islam in the Contemporary World*. Chapel Hill, NC: University of North Carolina Press, 2003.
Esme, Floyd. *1001 Little Ways to Save our Planet: Shortcuts to Feeling Good, Looking Great and Living Healthy*. London: Carlton Books, 2007.

Bibliography

Dolan, Jay P. *The American Catholic Experience. A History from the Colonial Times to the Present.* Garden City, NY: Doubleday, 1985.

Dupuis, Jacques. *Toward a Christian Theology of Religious Pluralism.* Maryknoll, NY: Orbis, 2001.

D'Antonio, William, Davidson, James, Hoge, Dean, Gautier, Mary. *American Catholics Today: New Realities of Their Faith and Their Church.* New York: Sheed and Ward, 2007.

Edwards, Denis. *Ecology at the Heart of Faith.* Maryknoll, NY: Orbis, 2006.

Fairbank, John King and Merle Goldman. *China.* Cambridge, MA: Harvard University Press, 2006.

Fiedler, Maureen and Linda Rabben, eds. *Rome Has Spoken.* New York: Crossroad, 1988.

Fisher, James T. *Communion of Immigrants: A History of Catholics in America.* New York: Oxford University Press, 2000.

Five Great Encyclicals. Edited by Gerald Treacy. New York: Paulist Press, 1939.

Flor y Cantu. Edited by John J. Limb, O. C. P. Portland, OR: O.C. Publications, 1989.

Foster, Lynn V. *A Brief History of Mexico.* New York: Facts on File, Inc., 1997

Gillis, Chester. *Roman Catholicism in America.* New York: Columbia University Press, 1999.

Gonzalez, Justo. *The Story of Christianity.* San Francisco: HarperCollins, 1984.

Griffen, Nigel. *Bartolome de Las Casas.* London: Penguin, 1992.

Haight, Roger. *Jesus, Symbol of God.* Maryknoll, NY: Orbis, 2001.

Hall, Suzanne, ed. *The People: Reflections of Native Peoples on the Catholic Experience in North America.* Washington, DC: National Catholic Educational Association, 1992.

Hanson, Victor Davis. *Mexifornia.* San Francisco: Encounter Books, 2003.

Hardon, John. *Modern Catholic Dictionary.* Garden City, NY: Doubleday and Co., 1980.

Harris, Sam. *The End of Faith: Religion, Terror, and the Future of Reason.* New York: W. W. Norton and Co., 2000.

Haught. John. *God and the New Atheism: A Critical Response to Dawkins, Harris, and Hitchens.* Louisville: Westminster John Knox Press, 2008.

Hennessey, James J. *American Catholics: A History of the Roman Catholic Community in the United States.* New York: Oxford University Press, 1981.

Hessler, Peter. *Oracle Bones: A Journey Between China's Past and Present.* New York: HarperCollins, 2006.

Hock, Ronald F. *The Social Context of Paul's Ministry: Tentmaking and Apostleship.* Minneapolis: Fortress Press, 2000.

Holland, Jack. *Misogyny: The World's Oldest Prejudice.* New York: Carroll & Graf Publishers, 2006.

Johnson, Paul. *A History of Christianity.* New York: Atheneum, 1979.

Jurgens, William. *The Faith of the Early Fathers.* Collegeville, MN: The Liturgical Press, 1970.

Kavanaugh, John. *Following Christ in a Consumer Society: The Spirituality of Cultural Resistance.* Maryknoll, NY: Orbis, 2006.

Keller, Albert. *Secularization.* New York: Herder and Herder, 1970.

Knowles, David, ed. "Introduction." In, *Augustine: The City of God*, vii–xxxiv. Translated by Henry Bettenson. New York: Penguin, 1972.

The Koran. New York: Random House, 1993.

Lakeland, Paul. *Postmodernity: Christian Identity in a Fragmented Age.* Minneapolis: Fortress Press, 1997.

Bibliography

Lazarus, Emma. *The Poems of Emma Lazarus*. 2 volumes. New York: MacMillan, 2007.

Martos, Joseph. *Doors to the Sacred: A Historical Introduction to Sacraments in the Catholic Church*. Garden City, NY: Doubleday and Co., 1982.

Modras, Ronald. *Ignatian Humanism: A Dynamic Spirituality for the 21st Century*. Chicago: Loyola Press, 2004.

Murphy, Cullen. *Are We Rome?: The Fall of an Empire and the Fate of America*. New York: Houghton Mifflin Co., 2007.

Nelson, Mike. *Stop Clutter from Wrecking your Family: Organize Your Children, Spouse, and Home*. Franklin Lakes: The Career Press, Inc., 2004.

The New Jerome Biblical Commentary. Edited by Joseph A. Fitzmeyer, Raymond E. Brown, and Roland E. Murphy. Englewood Cliffs, N.J.: Prentice Hall, Inc. 1990.

Nickle, Keith. *The Collection: A Study in Paul's Strategy*. London: SCM Press, 1966.

O'Brien, T.C. ed. *The Encyclopedic Dictionary of the Western Churches*. Washington, DC: Corpus Publications, 1970.

Pastoral Letters of the United States Catholic Bishops. 6 volumes. Edited by Hugh J. Nolan and Patrick Carey. Washington, DC: National Conference of Catholic Bishops, 1981–1987.

Peelman, Achiel. *Christ is a Native American*. Maryknoll, NY: Orbis, 1995.

Perkins, John. *Confessions of an Economic Hit Man*. San Francisco: Berrett-Koehler Publishers, 2004.

———. *The Secret History of the American Empire: Economic Hit Men, Jackals, and the Truth about Global Corruption*. New York: Dutton, 2007.

Phan, Peter. *Being Religious Interreligiously: Asian Perspectives on Interfaith Dialogue*. Maryknoll, NY: Orbis, 2004.

Rahner, Karl, ed. *Sacramentum Mundi*

Ramos, Jorge. *No borders: A Journalist's Search for Home*. Translated by Patricia J. Duncan. New York: HarperCollins, 2002.

———. *The Latino Wave: How Hispanics are Transforming Politics in America*. Translated by Ezra Fitz. New York: HarperCollins, 2005.

Renard, John. *101 Questions and Answers on Islam*. New York: Gramercy Press, 1998.

———. *Responses to 101 Questions on Buddhism*. Mahwah, NJ: Paulist Press, 1999.

———. *The Handy Religion Answer Book*. Detroit: Visible Ink Press, 2002.

Sandoval, Moises. *On the Move: A History of the Hispanic Church in the United States*. 2nd ed. Maryknoll, NY: Orbis, 2006.

Shorter, Aylward. *Toward a Theology of Enculturation*. Eugene, OR: Wipf & Stock, 1999.

Starkloff, Carl F. *A Theology of the In-Between: The Value of Syncretic Process*. Milwaukee: Marquette University Press, 2002.

———. *The People of the Center American Indian Religion and Christianity*. New York: Seabury Press, 1974.

Steinfels, Margaret O'Brien, ed. *American Catholicism and Civic Engagement*. New York: Rowman and Littlefield Publishers, Inc., 2004.

Stourton, Edward. *Paul of Tarsus: A Visionary Life*. Mahwah, NJ: Hidden Spring, 2004.

Tanner, Norman. *The Church and the World*. Mahwah, NJ: Paulist Press, 2005.

Tilley, Terrence. *Postmodern Theologies: The Challenge of Religious Diversity*. Maryknoll, N.Y. Orbis, 1995.

United States Conference of Catholic Bishops. *Co-Workers in the Vineyard of the Lord*. Washington, DC: U.S. Conference of Catholic Bishops, 2005.

———. *Strangers no Longer* (Washington, DC: U.S. Conference of Catholic Bishops, 2003.

Bibliography

Vasiliev, A.A. *History of the Byzantine Empire, 324-1453*. 2nd edition. 2 volumes. Milwaukee: The University of Wisconsin Press, 1964.

Vickery, Paul. *Bartolome de las Casas: Great Prophet of the Americas*. Mahwah, NJ: Paulist Press, 2006.

Vorgrimler, Herbert, ed. *Commentary on the Documents of Vatican II*. New York: Crossroad, 1989.

Wittgenstein, Ludwig. *Tractus Logico-Philosophicus*. London: Routledge, 2001.

Articles

Aquino, Maria Pilar. "Theology and Indigenous Cultures of the Americas: Conditions of Dialogue." *Catholic Theological Society of America Proceedings* 61/5 (2006): 19–50.

Bacevich, Andrew J. "The Cult of National Security." *Commonweal* 133/2 (January 2006): 8–9.

———. "Twilight of the Republic." *Commonweal* 133/21 (December 2006): 10–16.

Campbell, Simone, SSS. "Beckoned by Grace." *Network Connection* 34/4 (July/August 2006): 3.

Catania, Sara. "A is for Afro." *Mother Jones* 31 (September-October 2006): 70–78.

Clatterbuck, Mark S. "Post Vatican II Inculturation Among Native North American Catholics: A Study in the Missiology of Fr. Carl Starkloff, S. J." *Missiology: An International Review* 31/2 (April 2003): 207–22.

Fox, Tom. "U.S. Asian Catholics Gather in D. C." *National Catholic Reporter*, 14 July 2006, 9–10.

Gettelman, Elizabeth. "No Sex Please, We're Organizing." *Mother Jones* 32 (July–August 2007): 20–21.

Guntzel, Jeff S. "Making Connections." *National Catholic Reporter*, 16 June 2006, 1a.

Jeffrey, Clara. "Poor Losers." *Mother Jones* 27 (July–August 2006): 19–22.

Kelley, Alexia. "Challenge of the Common Good." *Network Connection* 34 (November–December 2006): 6–7.

Mulhall, Daniel S. "Building Inclusive Communities." *America* 196 (5 February 2007): 21–22.

Peñalver, Eduardo Moisés. "Are the Illegal Immigrants Pioneers? The Irony of American History." *Commonweal* 133 (5 May 2006): 9–10.

Pfaff, William. "Clash of Cultures." *Commonweal* 133/13 (June 2006): 11–15.

Pineda, Ana María. "Evangelization of the 'New World': A New World Perspective." *Missiology: An International Review* 20/2 (April 1992): 151–61.

———. "The Oral Tradition of a People: Forjadora de Rostro y Corazón." In, *Hispanic/Latino Theology. Challenge and Promise*, 104–116. Edited by Ada María Isasi-Diaz and Fernando F. Segovia. Minneapolis: Fortress Press, 1996.

Trautman, Brian. "How Accessible Are the New Mass Translations?" *America* 18 (21 May 2007): 10–11.*Films*

Dying to Live: A Migrant's Journey (Notre Dame, IN: Latino Spirituality and Culture, 2005), DVD.

Subject/Name Index

abortion, 53–54, 89–90
accountability
    keeping community and culture
        together, 102
    for providing quality education, 104
    vertical and horizontal dimensions
        of, 102–3
adaptation, 122
Ad Gentes (Vatican II), 155–56
African Council, 118, 122
African culture, Church's respect for, 119
aggiornamento, 40–41
Alexander VI, 130
Alternatives for Simple Living, 88
Amerindia, 153
Anna, Santa, 29
anointing, purposes of, 83–84
"Añoranza" (Yearning) (Rademacher), 141–45
Antioch, 2
anti-Semitism, 38–40, 44
Aquinas, Thomas, 55, 66, 117
Aquino, María Pilar, 146–58
Are We Rome? (Murphy), 72
Aristotle, 54–55, 66, 129–30
Armstrong, Karen, 24–25
Arrup, Pedro, 111
arts, used in addressing culture, 101–2
assimilation, vs. separatism, 28, 34–36
auctoritas (authority), 56
Augustine, 51–52, 99, 117
autochthonous churches, 155–56, 159

Bacevich, Andrew, 63, 71
base communities, 124
Beethoven, Ludwig von, 101
behavior, acceptable, 104–5
Benedict, Ruth, 89
Benedict XIV, 15–16, 18
Benedict XVI, 37, 61
Bible, incorporating surrounding culture
    into text, 116–17
birth control, 49
bishops, disagreements among, during
    development of *Pastoral
    Constitution*, 48–49
Bonhoeffer, Dietrich, 39
Book of Rites (Confucius), 57
border patrol, 34
boycotts, 94–95
Brockey, Liam, 16–17
Brothers and Sisters to Us (U.S. Bishops), 78
"Building Peace: A Pastoral Reflection on
    the Response to *The Challenge of
    Peace*" (U.S. Bishops), 103–4

Camara, Helder, 48
Cantor, Norman, 130–31
capitalism, 80–81, 94–95
Carrasco, Bartolomé, 152
caste systems, 45
Catholic Alliance for the Common
    Good, 65–66
Catholic Church
    anti-Semitism of, 38–40, 44
    comfortable with visions of saints, 22
    concern with internal affairs, 47–48
    confessing its mistakes to Mexican
        immigrants, 36

Catholic Church - continued
    different after Vatican II, xiv
    discretion required for, 44
    distinguishing between dogma and
        discipline in, 13
    end of attachment to European form
        of Catholicism, 16
    enriched by intermingling cultures,
        115–16
    examining interior of, xx
    failures and successes of, in dealing
        with other cultures, 10
    gender issue in, 58
    global mission of, 118–19
    good early relationship with Islam,
        22
    interaction with Muslims (1095–
        1291), 22–25
    new language for, 109
    new ministries in, 137
    in over-against mode, 44–45
    responding to multiculturalism,
        xiii–xiv, xix–xx, 3–4
    response to Latino/a immigration,
        31–33
    supporting diverse rites of worship,
        119
    vulnerable to cultural "-isms," 44
    Women's Ordination Conference, 58
    women's progress in, 58
celibacy, as discipline, 13
Center of Popular Theology, 153
change agents, 137
Charles V (king of Spain), 29, 128
Cheney, Dick, 74
China
    Catholic Church's presence in, 11–19
    Christian religion outlawed in, 16
    Hundred Flowers Campaign, 115
    increasing interest in, 11
    Jesuits in, 11–12, 13–18
    language of, 17, 18
    misogyny in, 57
Chinese Liturgy, 13, 15
Chinese Rites Controversy, 15–19
Chittister, Joan, 87
Christianity
    no borders within, 9
    spreading misogyny, 55
Christian Scholars Group on Christian-
    Jewish Relations, 42–43
Christian West, struggle with the
    Muslims, 75–76
Christ Is a Native American (Peelman),
    147
Chrysostom, John, Saint, 38
Church-State relations, in medieval
    period, 128–29, 130
Cinco de Mayo, 30
City of God (Augustine), 99
climate change, 76
Clutterless Recovery Groups, Inc., 88
Code of Canon Law, 117, 118
Colombo, Cardinal, 107
Commodity Form of Life, 62, 64
common good
    lacking awareness of, 64–66
    lost to privatized space, 60
common law, code of, 118
common sense philosophical movement,
    67
communities
    building within the parish, 125–26
    interfaith intercultural, 124–26
community
    building of, used in addressing
        culture, 106
    power in, 87
    principle of, 90–91
Confucianism, 14
Confucius, 57
consumerism, 61–64, 87–88
contemplation, used in addressing
    culture, 109–10
Corinth, divisions in church at, 8
corporatocracy, 74–75
Cortés, Hernan, 28, 131
Council of Basil, 38–39
Council of Clermont, 24
Council of Elvira, 39–40, 89
Council of Nicaea, 45
Council of Trent, 18, 45, 117
"Co-Workers in the Vineyard of the
    Lord" (U.S. Bishops), 137

creation
    continual process of, 76–77
    goodness of, 51
    humans as partners in, 92–93
    precious nature of, 93
    spiritual dimension of, 76
    stories of, 116
Crusades
    anti-Jewish sentiment during, 38
    continuing effect of, 24–25
    necessity of understanding context for, 20
    reasons for, 23–24
    review of, 24
cultural conditioning, 86
culture
    clash of, 75–76
    defining, 2–4
    diagnosing problems within, 50–51
    diagnosing sickness in, 51–52
    equality among, 72–73
    faith-filled, 114
    healing, 84–85
    including human social community, 51
    Jewish, in Jesus' time, 113–14
    none preferred before God, 5
    refining and developing, 100
    responding to, 3–4
    of the Roman Empire, 113–14
    showing respect for, 17–18
    threefold perspective on, 3
    U.S., fluidity of, 4

Dearden, Cardinal, 49
death penalty, 90
Declaration of the Church to Non-Christian Religions. See Nostra Aetate
Decree on Ecumenism (Vatican II), 25, 124
democracy, losing sense of accountability, 96
Descartes, René, 66
dialogue, 108
    energizing the healing process, 87
    importance of, 123–24
    interreligious, 43–44
    mutual recognition of parties involved, 154–55
    used in addressing culture, 100–101
Didache (*Teaching of the Twelve Apostles*), 89
discipline, 13, 18
divine revelation, intercultural matrix of, 114
dogma, 13, 18
Dogmatic Constitution on the Church (Vatican II), xix
dualism, 51
dualistic fundamentalism, 67

early Church
    anti-Semitism in, 38
    defining itself over against Rabbinic Judaism, 45
    multiculturalism forming basis of, 6
    responding to multiculturalism, xv
    unity of community within, 7–8
    women's role in, 7
ecology, 76–77, 92–94
Ecumenical Association of Third World Theologians, 152
education, used in addressing culture, 104–5
Edwards, Denis, 93
Eisenhower, Dwight, 71
empiricism, 66–67, 91–92
encomienda system, 132
enculturation, 116–19
    broad application of, 11
    defined, 111, 112
    imperial connotation of, 115
    new approach to, xiv
    parish's important role in, 19
English Liturgy, better translation of, 122–23
Episcopal Church, ordaining women as bishops, 58
Eucharist, as discipline, 13
Eucharistic prayers, in different countries, 119
evidence, 67

evil, not using as means to achieve good, 86
Ex quo singulari (Benedict XIV), 15–16

failure, providing occasion for improvement, 10
faith
   elimination of, 67
   transforming or developing culture, 112–16
family, 49
Farías, José Llaguno, 152
Farrakhan, Louis, 40
Felici, Archbishop, 49
female infanticide, 56
fiscal policy, 74
Flores, Patricio, 36
Floyd, Esme, 94
foot binding, 57
Fourth Lateran Council, 40
France, invasion of Mexico, 30
freedom, used in addressing culture, 106–7

Germany, during World War II, 39
global consciousness, 95
global environment, 53
globalization, 131
global warming, 76
God, inculturated in Jewish culture, 113
Good Friday prayer, changes to, 37
grace, 51, 85, 86, 100, 114
Gratian, 117–18
Gregorian Reform, 24
Gregory VII, 23–24, 117, 118

Hadith, 20
Haight, Roger, xiv, 52–53
Halliburton, 74
Hanson, Victor Davis, 4, 27–28
Harmony of Discordant Canons (Gratian), 117–18
Harris, Sam, 67
healing, general principles of, 85–87
Heifer International, 88
heresy, good in, 45

Hermes, 108
Hernández, E. López, 149
Hidalgo, Miguel, 29
Hip-Hop Caucus, 103
Hitler, Adolf, 39–40
hoarding, 64
Hock, Ronald, 1–2
Holland, rites of women in, 57
hospitality, 5, 39, 114
Humanae Vitae (Paul VI), 49
human condition, refining, 99–100
Humane Borders, 34
humans, dignity of, 52–53
Hume, David, 66
Hundred Flowers Campaign, 115

idolatry, 61–62
immigrants, welcome to, xv–xvi
immigration
   root of pluralistic society, 79
   undocumented, 31
imperialism, 70–71, 72–75
   by-products of, 131
   in Spanish culture, 130–31
Incarnation
   mystery of, 114
   as unchangeable dogma, 13
Inconvenient Truth, An, 94
inculturation
   blessings of, 121
   defined, 111, 112
   difficult in individualistic culture, 123
   as historical process, 118
   as interculturation, 121, 123–24
   language's role in, 121–23
   as two-way process, 118–19
   universal Church, needing detachment from its own internal culture, 118
   as Word's outward expression, 119
Indigenous communities, in the Americas, Church's reconciliation with, 156–59
Indigenous theology, insufficiently addressed, 147–48
individualism, 60–61, 90–91

Subject/Name Index   169

inductive method, 48–49
Inquisition, 129
interculturation, 73
   concern with, 115
   inculturation as, 121, 123–24
   prerequisite for, 133
   interfaith intercultural communities, 124–26
International Association of Catholic Missiologists, 153
interreligious dialogue,
   recommendations for, 43–44
Islam
   good early relationship with Catholic Church, 22
   origins of, 20–21
   pillars of the faith, 21–22
   similarities with Christian tradition, 22
Israel, new Christian community depicted as, 7–8
Iturbide, Augustin de, 29–30

Jerusalem, as sacred Muslim city, 22–23
Jesuits
   Jesuit Volunteers, 106
   mission into China, 11–12, 13–18
   practicing missionary accommodation, 12
Jesus
   crucifixion and resurrection of, 114
   historical, 113
   integrated into Jewish tradition of his time, 42
   interpreting message of, within appropriate cultural context, 117
   viewing, within cultural context, 148–49
Jews
   call to convert to Christianity, 37
   changing Catholic attitude toward, 40–43
   ghettoes for, 38–39
   under Hitler's reign, 39–40
   referred to as faithless in former Good Friday liturgy, 37
   subject to anti-Semitism from the Church, 38–40
jihad, 21
John Paul II, 76
   repudiating all persecution of the Jews, 41–42
   theology of the body, 95
John XXIII, xix, 49, 121–22
   program of *aggiornamento*, 40–41
   removing *Judaicam perfidiam* from Good Friday liturgy, 37
Johnson, Paul, 128
Journey to the East: The Jesuit Mission to China, 1579–1724 (Brockey), 16–17
Juarez, Benito, 30

Kavanaugh, John, 3, 61–64
King, Martin Luther, 31, 77, 156
Knowles, David, 117

labor issues, 65
Lamm, Richard, 28
language
   role of, in inculturation, 121–23
   used in addressing culture, 108–9
La Raza, 35
Las Casas, Bartolomé de, 127, 130
   as protector of native peoples, 133–35
   reporting on violence of Spanish conquistadores, 131–33
Latin American Confederation of Religious Communities, 152
Latin American Council of Bishops, 152
Latin American Council of Churches, 152
Latin American Ecumenical Articulation of Indigenous Pastoral, 152
Latin Mass, attachment to, 15
Latino culture, addressing presence of, in United States, 27–28
Latin Rite, 18, 117
Lavigerie, Cardinal, 119
Leo XIII, 65
Lercaro, Cardinal, 48, 69–70, 109
life, sacredness of, 90

liturgical languages, multiplication of, 18–19
Locke, John, 66
Lombard, Peter, 58
Lona, Arturo, 152

Maier, Charles, 63
Malines Text, 47
marriage, 49
Martos, Joseph, 84
Mexico
    history of, 28–31
    indigenous churches in, 118
    polarized between Church and government, 30
    War for Independence in, 29
Mexifornia (Hanson), 27–28
militarism, 70–72
ministry, new kinds of, 137–38
misogyny, 54–60, 97
mission, measuring success or failure of, 12
missionaries, tutoring indigenous replacements, 123
missionary accommodation, 12–15
Missionary Indigenous Council, 153
moral education, 105
Morales, Evo, 6
Moreles, Jose, 29
Mozart, Amadeus, 101
Muawiya, 23
Muhammad, 20, 21
Muhammadanism. *See* Islam
Mulhall, David S., 125
multicultural context, churches' need to engage in dialogue about, 43
multiculturalism, support and development of, 138–39
Murphy, Cullen, 72
Muslims
    Catholic interaction with (1095–1291), 22–25
    contemporary view of, 19–20
    Holy Land of, 23
    reconciling with, 25
    struggle with the Christian West, 75–76
    viewing Holy Wars as self-defense, 23

National Center of Assistance to Indigenous Missions, 153
National Coordination of Indigenous Pastoral, 153
Nation of Islam, 40
Nelson, Mike, 88
Nicholas V, 130
Nickle, Keith, 7–8
No Borders (Ramos), 36
Nostra Aetate (Vatican II), 11, 41, 124
Nuremberg laws, 40

oil
    as biblical symbol, 83–84
    in patristic period, 84
Olmec culture, 28
ordination, Sacrament of, 58
Origen, 38
Ovalle, Julio Cabrera, 152

Pastoral Andean Institute, 153
Pastoral Constitution on the Church in the Modern World, The (Vatican II), xix, 44, 104–9, 120, 121, 137
    brief history of, 47–50
    on culture, 3, 50
patriarchy, 56, 97
Paul, Apostle
    applying principles of indigenous leadership, 6–7
    dealing with multiple cultures on his missionary journeys, 2, 4–6
    letters of, instructive in dealing with U.S. immigrants, 4–6
    life of, 1–2
    on significance of the risen Christ, 59
    taking up collection for saints in Jerusalem, 7–8
    using image of Body of Christ, 8
Paul V, 13, 15
Paul VI, 49
Pawlikowski, John, 42
Pax Christi, 103
peacemaking, used in addressing culture, 103–4
Peelman, Achiel, 147
People of the Center, The (Starkloff), 147

People of God, xix
Perkins, John, 73–75
Peter, Apostle, 5–6
Pfaff, William, 75
Phan, Peter, 121
Phoebe, 7
Pineda, Ana María, 147–48, 150
Pius IX, 129
Pius XI, 16, 65
Pius XII, 16, 39
Plan of Córdoba, 29
Plato, 99, 101, 106
Plotinus, 117
pluralism, 79–80
    accepting reality of, xiv
    theological, 122
political involvement, 138–39
political order, 96
Polk, James, 29
Pontifical Council for Interreligious Dialogue and the Congregation of Peoples, 43–44
Pope, Stephen J., 78
postmodernity, xiv, 52–53
potestas (power), 56
poverty, 69–70
    Church's need to move toward, 48, 69–70
power
    expansion of, 131
    speaking truth to, 138
privacy, as new gospel, 60
pro-life, 90
"Proper Development of Culture" (Vatican II), 46, 47, 51
Protocols of the Elders of Zion, 40
purpose, for men and women, 55

Quadragesimo Anno (Pius XI), 65
Qur'an, 20, 22

racism, 77–78, 88–89
Ramazzini, Alvaro, 152
Ramos, Jorge, 36
rationalism, 70
Reform Laws (Mexico), 30
relativism, 61, 91

religion, separating from a particular culture, 19
religious pluralism, 79
Renew Programs, 124
Rerum Novarum (Leo XIII), 65
research, scientific, used in addressing culture, 105
Reyes, G. López, 151–52
Ricci, Matteo, 11–12, 14, 16, 18
risen Lord, not bound to a single culture, 118
rites, local, 15, 119
Roman Empire, 113–14
Roman Empire, misogyny in, 56
Rome, gulf separating, from missionaries in the field, 18
Romulus, 56
Ruiz, Samuel, 152

Salvation Army, 88
scholastic theology, 117
scientific research, 105
Scott, Winfield, 30
Second Vatican Council, xix, 40–41, 124–25
    addressing Church-state relations, 129
    reducing risk of repeating historical failures, 46
secularism, 67–68
separatism, vs. assimilation, 28, 34–36
sexuality, human, 95–96
sexual revolution, 57
Short Account of the Destruction of the Indies (Las Casas), 132–33
silence, importance of, 155
slavery, Christian tradition supporting, 129–30
society, role of, in caring for the common good, 65
Socrates, 99, 101
Spain
    activities of the conquistadores, 28–29, 30–31, 45, 131–33. See *also* Mexico
    sixteenth-century culture of, 128–29
spirit, human, cultivation of, 109–10

Subject/Name Index

Stalin, Joseph, 101
Starkloff, Carl, 147, 159
state, role of, in caring for the common good, 65
Stourton, Edward, 2
Strangers No Longer: Together on the Journey of Hope (U.S. and Mexican bishops), 32–33, 34
St. Vincent de Paul Society, 88
subjectivism, 68–69
Suenens, Cardinal, 47
Summa Theologica (Aquinas), 55, 117
Sunna, 20
Sybel, H., 23
"Syllabus of Errors" (Pius IX), 129
syncretic religion, in Mexico, 29

Temple of the Resurrection, destruction of, 22–23
tension, felt, in healing wounded culture, 86
tent making, in Paul's time, 1–2
Teología India, 148–56
theologian, function of, 149–51
theology
    of the body, 95
    expressing itself through various cultures, 122
    of liberation, 151
    systematized, 148
Theology of the In-Between, The; The Value of Syncretic Process (Starkloff), 147
Third Latin American Encounter of *Teología India*, 154
Thompson, Francis, 139
Timothy, 6–7
Titus, 7
Trautman, Donald, 122–23
treaty of Guadalupe Hidalgo, 30
truth
    not restricted to the Catholic Church, 107–8
    search for, used in addressing culture, 107–8

United Nations, fighting discrimination against women, 58–59
United States
    awareness of Catholic cultural diversity in, 10
    corporate culture of, 73–74
    as empire, 72–74, 131
    immigration system of, 33–34
    Latino/a immigration to, reasons behind, 31
    legalizing undocumented workers in, 33
    mingling of cultures in, 115
    misogyny in, 57–58
    settlement of, by illegal squatters, 33
    treatment of immigrants in, by descendants of immigrants, 133
    war with Mexico, 30
    women's suffrage in, 58
Urban II, 23, 24, 128

Vera, Raúl, 152
visions, 22
visual language, 109

Ward, Barbara, 49
water, as biblical symbol, 83
Wittgenstein, Ludwig, 108
Wojtyla, Karol, 47. *See also* John Paul II
WomanChurch, 58
women, role of, 96–97. *See also* misogyny

Zaire Mass, 119
Zimbabwe funeral rite, 119
Zurich Text, 47